POP YOUR PARADIGM!

Neutralize your "programming" and start LIVING your life!

By Sandra Anne Daly

Scottsdale Arizona
www.inkwellproductions.com

Copyright © 2009
By Sandra Anne Daly

First printing 2009
All rights reserved

No part of this book may be reproduced in any form or by any means without the permission in writing from the publisher.

ISBN: 978-0-9814648-7-9
Library of Congress Control Number: 2009931294

Published by Inkwell Productions
10869 N. Scottsdale Road # 103-128
Scottsdale, AZ 85254-5280
Tel. 480-315-3781
E-mail info@inkwellproductions.com
Website www.inkwellproductions.com
Printed in the United States of America

Cover illustration by Timothy Wood

*This book is dedicated to
Carol Elaine Bachelor, my mom.
She lived her entire life at the mercy
of her "programming," and she died
without ever discovering that her life
did not have to be the way it was.
I know that she's looking happily on
from her place on a higher plane — both
proud of me, and excited for me,
because I did make that discovery,
and then I changed my whole life.*

Table of Contents

Introduction vii

Chapter 1: Surviving My Life 3

Chapter 2: The Life and Times of a Paradigm 13

Chapter 3: The Adventure Begins 27

Chapter 4: Peace Begins With Me 53

Chapter 5: Goodbye, Old Life 67

Chapter 6: The (Bus) Ride of My Life! 81

Chapter 7: A Brand New Me 117

Chapter 8: Hello, New Life! 139

Chapter 9: One Step (in Faith) at a Time 155

Chapter 10: Freedom, Fear, and Letting Go 171

Chapter 11: Loneliness, Successes and
            Non-prostitution 183

Chapter 12: A Happy Ending? 193

In Gratitude 196

Introduction

When I wrote the main body of this book, I had no idea what the word "paradigm" (pronounced "para-dime") meant. I had heard it before, but I just thought of it as some New Age buzz word and I saw no need to spend any time trying to understand it. After all, what could it possibly have to do with me?

And then, in September of 2008, almost exactly nine years to the day from the day that I saved my own life by turning on my television, I learned what paradigms are and how they work. And I learned these things from the exact same Teacher I had found on TV nine years previously! Coincidence? I think not.

What I learned in September of 2008 from my Teacher was that the entire story that I'm sharing with you, this whole book, is about a paradigm that I had lived at the mercy of for most of my life. It's about how it was created in me as a very small child, reinforced in me throughout my subsequent childhood years, and then unknowingly lived by me for more than thirty-four years.

Far more importantly, though, it's about how I was able to neutralize that paradigm, despite the fact that

I had never even heard the word before. In experiencing the process of neutralizing the programming I had unknowingly lived my whole life from, I became a completely different—much "bigger"—person, and I began to actually *live* my life the way it was meant to be lived! It was an incredible experience, and I feel both blessed and privileged to be able to share it with you.

This is my story, but it's also everyone's story, because we all have paradigms that very effectively control our lives until we find a way to disable them. This book is the story of how I changed my life by changing my habits of thought. But it is also a great example of how you can do the same thing for yourself if you are not happy with your life the way it is.

Do you know what a paradigm is? Do you care? I think that gaining an understanding of paradigms is the greatest gift that anyone could ever give to themselves, because if we don't know what they are—or even that they are there—we are completely powerless to change our lives for the better if we should want to do so. The following is an explanation of what a paradigm is, and how a paradigm works, that is easy for anyone to understand and relate to his or her own life:

What is a paradigm?

A paradigm is a personal belief, or system of beliefs, which behaves like an incredibly powerful program running in the background of a person's thought processes. Every choice, every attitude, every decision, every behavior, every action a person takes is dictated by whatever the paradigm perceives to be "true." There are paradigms which have a negative influence on a person's thought processes, just as there are paradigms that influence in a positive way. And there is not a person on planet Earth who does *not* have paradigms, as they are an unavoidable aspect of the human experience.

A negative paradigm behaves like a tyrant, controlling every thought a person thinks and every move a person makes. If that person tries to do something that doesn't agree with the paradigm (something "outside the box"), that tyrant ensures that he or she knows that what they want to do is just "not meant to be" for them. The tyrant makes sure that person regrets ever thinking they might be able to change anything about their life. The tyrant creates situations that can be seen as "proof" that what the person wants can never happen for them. The tyrant makes life so uncomfortable that the person must give up on their Dreams just to get some relief from the feelings of fear, frustration, and pain that the tyrant is so very skilled at creating. As the person gives up, the pressure from the tyrant is relieved, and the person goes back to settling for the limited life that is in the comfort zone of the paradigm. This tyrant says to the person, "Dream? You will never live your Dream. You are worthless, and bad, and you do not deserve to live the life you really want. Stay in your box where you are safe. If you try to leave it, you could be hurt or humiliated. You might make a mistake, and then everyone would know how clumsy and undeserving you are. No, you're better off stuck right here where I can keep you safe from yourself." The negative paradigm is what's behind self-sabotage, self-defeating behaviors, and choices the person makes that he or she *knows* are unhealthy, but that they just can't seem to keep from making.

On the other hand, a positive paradigm is like a true friend: supportive and encouraging. It's a friend that knows the person's strength, wisdom, and value.

It's a friend, joyfully cheering that person on as they take baby steps, giant strides, or leaps and bounds toward the life they want to be living. It's a friend that says, "You are loved. You are worthy. You deserve to live your Dreams and I support you in all ways."

Who has paradigms?

We all have paradigms—both the positive ones that say, "I love you just as you are and I support you on your path to becoming what you want to be." And the negative ones that say, "Not only are you not worthy of your Dreams, but you must live afraid. No change will be allowed, and if you try you will fail and then I'll make sure you feel even worse."

Which type of paradigm is more dominant within you? The limiting type? Or the type that makes you feel free and joyful and powerful and able to create what you want in your life? You can tell by the way you feel which one you experience the most often and the most powerfully.

If you most often feel as if the world—or even life itself—is against you, then you can be assured that you are under the thumb of the tyrant.

On the other hand, if you most often feel whole and powerful and joyful—congratulations! You are walking side by side with the most supportive and loving friend you will ever have!

To shift a paradigm

If you find that you're now just existing, or surviving, under the thumb of the tyrant, I have great news! You are by no means doomed to live out your days under the rule of that tyrant. The only reason you have been there this long is that you did not know the paradigm existed, manipulating your life from its hiding place in your subconscious. But now you do. And now that you know it's there, you'll begin to recognize its sly little tricks and traps for what they are. And you'll begin taking your power back from the tyrant, so you can apply it toward the joyful, expanded life of your Dreams. You'll begin to be your own friend. You'll begin to learn to shift your attention to that loving and supportive friend who has always been there, wanting to help you reach your Dreams, but whose voice has been drowned out by the tyrant.

All it takes to shift a paradigm is to shift your attention from thoughts of limitation and, "I can't," to thoughts of freedom and, "I can do anything!" Yes, that's all it takes, but it will also take your all, because the tyrant is not going to easily give up its power over you. It's not going to fade quietly into the background and disappear. No, it's going to hang on for dear life, kicking and screaming and throwing fits. It's going to do everything it can to keep you under its thumb, where it feels you belong. In fact, it knows that its very life depends on keeping you there.

The shifting of a paradigm may just be one of the most uncomfortable things you will ever do. But the shifting of the paradigm will — without any question at all — be one of the most liberating things you will ever do.

In September of 1999, I was thirty-four years old and living a life in which I fully expected to be dead at some point before my fortieth birthday, remembered only as one more statistic of domestic violence.

Today, rather than being just a memory, I find that my life is amazing and incredible, filled with all sorts of wonderful things. Things like joy and growth, love and inspiration, acceptance and peace. I no longer simply "survive my life." I no longer live at the mercy of my programming. I have learned how to live my Dreams. I have learned how to neutralize the tyrant and allow myself to create the life that I want to be living.

When I began the journey described in this book I had no idea that I was living my life by default. I was completely unaware of what I was really thinking. Actually, it would be more accurate to say that I did not understand that I wasn't really "thinking" at all — I was running a program. I was completely oblivious to my own habits and patterns of thought, and I had no clue that those habits of thought were influencing my entire life and every single thing I ever experienced.

When something has become a habit, this means that we do it automatically, without being consciously aware of what we're doing. And when we've developed a particular habit of thought, that habit of thought becomes a belief, which in turn becomes a program running powerfully in the background of our mind. It becomes a paradigm. And this paradigm influences *everything* that we live!

When I wrote the main body of this manuscript, I had no clue as to the meaning of the word "paradigm." All I knew was that I had completely changed my life by deliberately changing the way I looked at and experienced things — by deliberately creating healthy new habits of thought to replace the old unhealthy ones that had previously shaped my life. I didn't know there was actually a word, or a term, for that. Now I do, though. Now I know that as I was creating new habits of thought, I was actually "shifting," or, "popping" a paradigm. *Pop Your Paradigm!* is actually a great description of the *process* of a paradigm shift. This book was deliberately written so that the reader can actually see what it's like to first become aware of the power your thoughts have over your entire life, then to learn to pay attention to what you're thinking, then to deliberately stop yourself in the middle of a pattern of thought that limits you, and finally to create a new habit of thought that is in harmony with "possibility," instead of "problem."

In order for you to understand just how huge this journey has been for me—just how profound that paradigm shift was—you need to understand what the first thirty-four years of my life were like. When you get a little bit of understanding about that, you will begin to know that no matter what your history looks like and no matter where you are right now, you can create a whole new life for yourself. No matter what place you're in right now—no matter what it looks like or feels like, you do not have to stay there. You can change your life from right where you are—if you wish to and if you make the choice to do so.

One word of warning: The beginning of this story is not pretty. Depending on what you think about certain things (what your beliefs, judgments, and prejudices may be), you may find some of the things that I have to say anywhere from a little uncomfortable to extremely offensive. I apologize in advance. But please understand that I am expressing how *I* felt and what was going on with *me* at that time. If you choose to take any of it personally, or if you choose to be offended or angered by it, well...that is entirely your choice and it is something that *you* own. As Dr. Wayne Dyer says, "You do not get to define me by judging me. In your judgment of me, you define yourself as a person who needs to judge." So please, just take my words for what they are, something I have lived, something I have experienced. I am speaking from my own perspective.

I began my story in such a way that the person reading it could get some sense of the negativity that was "normal" for me for such a long time. But I chose not to go into a lot of detail about the negative because that would serve no purpose. If you've lived the same kind of life that I have, then you can probably make your own guesses and fill in the gaps quite accurately. If you *haven't* lived the same kind of life that I have, then I can pretty much guarantee that you don't want those gaps filled in. That would only serve to make you sad, or to feel bad for me, and that is not what I want this book to be about. I began there because that is where this story began. That's where and when the "programming" happened. That is where and how the paradigm was created.

Pop Your Paradigm! is a description of the process I used to completely change my life. It's about how I went from living a life of only limitation, to learning that it was okay for me to dare to dream, to learning *how* to dream, to living the life of my dreams.

This hasn't been just a journey — it has been a fun, sometimes terrifying, almost always joyous adventure and I want to share it with everyone. There are so many people out there with the belief that they can never have what they really want in their lives. I am living proof that no matter what has happened to you in your past, you can make both your present and your future whatever you want them to be!

This story is an example of the *process* of learning how to change the way you look at and experience your life. Because it is a process, I have included my thought processes along the way, so the reader can see that it's not only *possible* to change your thinking, but that it MUST be an internal, conscious, deliberate and determined changing of habits of thought. You will see as you get into this book that my thought processes would begin in "victim" mode (the paradigm) and I would have to consciously remember, "Oh yeah. I don't like how this feels. I don't like where this thought will take me. What's a thought that feels better?" And you will also see that the most difficult part of this was first remembering to do it, and then being willing to let go of habits of thought that did not serve me. And, hopefully, you will see from my example that no matter who you are or what your circumstances, you can change your life if you choose to do so.

Please join me in the first steps of my Great Adventure…

The Birth of a Paradigm

Chapter I

Surviving My Life

*"Experience, which destroys innocence,
also leads one back to it."*
~ James Baldwin

Sometimes I get a little irritated when I hear ministers or speakers say, "Go back to when you were a child and you knew there were no limits to what you could do." I know they mean well, and they make a good point for probably the majority of people, but what about those of us who didn't have that kind of happy, seemingly limitless childhood? What about those of us who spent our childhood trying desperately to protect ourselves and/or our siblings from an abusive person or persons? People who have that kind of history are not able to "go back to when we had no limits" because we are not able to remember a time when we were able to think big.

There were only two things for me as a child: There was pain, and there was wondering when something painful was going to happen again. There were no dreams and there was always the box of limitation that I lived in.

Following are a few examples of things I experienced at different points throughout my life:

Early childhood (up to age 5):
Why does my mommy sleep all the time?
And why does she smell like that?
Why is my mom gone to the hospital again?
Why does he (not my father) touch me in places that make me uncomfortable and nervous?

Why does she (his wife) let him get into the bathtub with me when she knows that I am afraid? And I never want her to leave the room, but she always does! She always leaves me alone with him even though she knows I'm afraid.

He says that what he does to me is okay because he's already been Saved. He says he doesn't need to worry that what he's doing is bad because Jesus died for his sins. It doesn't feel okay to me. I am uncomfortable and nervous. I can't sleep. What if he does it again? I don't want to wake up with his hands in my panties any more. Why would Jesus say that it's okay for me to be hurt like this? Maybe I'm bad.

Age 5 to 8:
My mom is gone again. They say she doesn't want me or love me anymore and that's why she left without me. What did I do wrong? Maybe I am as bad as they say I am.

Fear, pain, and humiliation are what I know.
They tell me that I am nothing.
They tell me that I am worthless.
They tell me that I am ugly and stupid.
They tell me that I have no value at all because I'm just a girl.

They are big and I am little — they must be right because they know so much more than I do. They tell me these things over and over again, so they must be true, right?

Deeper fear, more pain, and malicious humiliation are my way of life.

I hate my life. I hate them.

Why did I have to be a girl?

Bruises. Welts. Pain.

Punishments for things I didn't do just because I'm a girl and I'm worthless, so why bother looking to find the truth? After all, *the boy* could never do anything wrong or bad, so it could only have been me… even though it *wasn't!* If only I was a boy, then my life wouldn't be like this.

Five, six, seven years old. I am forced to take off all my clothes and dance naked for a group of teenaged boys. They laugh. I am humiliated and afraid and I hate them.

Five, six, seven years old. I am forced to strip once again. This time I must sit naked on the piano bench while that same group of teenagers spits loogies at me from across the room. They tell me this is what I'm here for—this is all I'm good for. I must sit completely still. I know from experience that I will be punished if I move. My long hair is plastered to my head and neck, full of spit and snot. I'm sitting with my legs tight together and my hands at my sides. There is a puddle of spit and snot in my lap. It overflows and drips down between my knees and puddles on the floor beneath me. One of those boys has really good aim and now there is a huge loogie hanging from the end of my nose. It just hangs there for the longest time while they all laugh and high five each other. I am completely humiliated and I begin to sob. I get punished for crying. After all, this is what I'm here for. This is why I was put on this earth. What the hell am I crying for? I am humiliated and angry and afraid. I hate them all and I hate myself.

I want my mom, but they say she left and went to California without me because she doesn't love me anymore. Why should she love me, anyway, when I'm so bad, and ugly, and stupid?

I hate my life. I hate myself. I hate them. Why did I have to be born if this is the way my life has to be?

Age 8-9:

It's a few days after my eighth birthday and a lady from Children's Services Division has come to take me from that house. She explains to me what a foster home is and she asks me if I'd like to go to one. I don't even have to think about it—I immediately say, "Yes!"

My father cries as she takes me by the hand and leads me away from the house. I have no idea what those tears are about. My father has allowed this abuse to go on for three years. Why is he crying as I leave?

The foster home. They act like they're nice, but I don't trust them. When are they going to hit me? Or touch me in uncomfortable places? Or tell me that I'm bad? I have to be ready. I have to be on guard at all times.

I have a friend who lives across the street. Her name is Phyllis. I haven't had a friend since before my mom went away. I'm not sure what to do…what if she finds out that I'm bad? I have to be on guard. But it sure is fun to swing on her swing set! She doesn't seem to care that I'm so ugly, and she doesn't seem to think I'm stupid, either. I'm still on guard, but I smile sometimes.

Four months have passed and they still haven't hurt me. I'm still afraid to relax, but it's getting a little easier. They always treat me as if they like me. I don't understand it. They say I'm pretty—I can't figure out why they would tell me that. They just haven't found out that I'm bad yet. Or maybe I'm not really bad? Maybe the people that I hate were wrong? I don't know. I still have to be on guard.

Another month has passed. I'm sitting on the couch looking out the front window and I see a woman walking up the sidewalk. I look a little closer. It's my MOM!! I pull on the front door so hard that it *flies* open and hits the wall from the force of my excitement. I have been told for the last three years that my mom is not there for me because I'm bad and she doesn't want me anymore. I have tried my hardest for those three years not to believe that. But I know what I see, and what I see is that she hasn't been there. And I see that it's the family members who are there and who are supposed to love me — they are the ones who tell me I'm bad and ugly and stupid and they treat me like I'm bad and ugly and stupid. Add those facts together and what do I get? I'm bad and ugly and stupid and if my mom really loved me I would have been with her for the last three years. And those three years would have been happy. But I don't care about all that right now. Right now what I know is that *my mom is HERE!* I run out to her and jump into her arms — she hugs me hard and she kisses my whole face and I don't ever want her to let go. *THIS* is what it feels like to be happy!

My mom wants to start a new life for herself — for us — so we move to South Carolina where she works, and we live, in a motel in Myrtle Beach. I am eight years old and for three months that summer I know what it's like for my life to be good!

Then she gets sick again. She has to go back to Oregon, to the hospital she's familiar with. She leaves me again. She leaves me in a foster home in South Carolina. The foster father is a Seventh Day Adventist pastor, and he is a mean, cruel man. He is worse than the people I hate. He says the reason my mom is crazy is that I am a child of the Devil. He says I must be punished. He hurts me for the next nine months, until his wife finally sneaks me out in the middle of the night. She has called my mother in Oregon and told her that if she ever wants to see me alive again, she'd better come and get me. So after nine months, my mom is back for me and, once again, I am happy. But I will never trust happiness again—it is not worth it. I am nine years old.

Reinforcing the Paradigm

Age 9 to adulthood:
The people I hate must have been right—maybe I'm just bad. Maybe I really don't deserve anything good. I hate my life. I am ugly. I am not worth anything. I desperately want to be loved, but I know that I don't deserve that.

My mom tells me that I'm special and I'm beautiful and that I can be anything I want to be. Whatever. She says that she loves me, and I believe her, but her dislike of herself and her depression are stronger and more powerful than her love for me. I watch her neglect herself. I watch her sabotage herself. I watch her treat herself as if she doesn't deserve to be happy. I watch her be a victim, and I learn from her that it's "normal" to be a victim. It's "normal" to be depressed. It's "normal" to live in poverty. It's "normal" to believe that no one will ever love you and that you can't love yourself, because, well, if no one else will ever love you then you must not be worth loving, right?

This is the mentality that I have as I grow up. I'm worthless. I'm ugly. No one will ever love me because

I'm not worth loving. I don't deserve to be happy or have anything good in my life.

Living the Paradigm

As I get older and become interested in boys I don't understand the ones who are nice to me. It must just be because they haven't figured out that I'm bad yet. I can't allow myself to be happy with them because I know how painful it will be when they start to be mean. So I just don't allow myself to get involved with "nice" boys. I am used to being treated badly — that is what I'm comfortable with because that is what I know, so those are the kind of guys that I attract into my life.

But I so desperately want to be loved!

Why did I have to be born if this is the way my life is always going to be? I hate my life and I hate myself.

Hey, I know! What if I have a baby? Then I will have someone to love and take care of. I would like to have a baby!

So now I am seventeen years old, married to a man who hates himself as much as I hate myself. And he says that he loves me, but he treats me as if he hates me. It doesn't matter. I'm pregnant, and that's what I wanted…

Now I'm nineteen and I have a daughter that I love very much, but my husband is going to kill me sooner or later if I stay with him. He has already attempted to run me over with the car once. It was pure luck that saved me that time. I live in fear of him trying again and succeeding. My luck is not good enough to save me twice. And then there's the gun. It's a .357 Magnum and my husband gets it out when he gets angry. I am afraid all the time, and he is angry all the time. I feel that it's only a matter of time before I will be dead at his hands. I finally decide that I can't take this fear any more. I take my daughter and run away to a battered women's shelter. They help me get a restraining order and they hand me welfare paperwork.

I am nineteen years old, with a two-year-old daughter. I am divorced and on welfare. I have no self-esteem. I have no self-confidence. I have no self-respect. I am ugly and I am worthless and I will never be happy.

I desperately want to be loved…

I love my daughter very much, but my depression and self-hatred are stronger and more powerful than my love for my daughter.

I so very desperately want to be loved.

(As I look back on this time of my life I see a pattern. I see that I lived my life in much the same way that my mother lived hers. Very depressed and desperately wanting to be loved by someone else, yet unable to see anything in myself that was worth loving.)

Adulthood:

Parties, alcohol, one relationship after another — desperately trying to find someone to love me.

Married again. Another child when I am twenty-two — a son this time. I love him very much, but my depression and self-hatred are stronger and more powerful than my love for my children.

I desperately want to be loved.

Parties, alcohol, lots of cocaine. Another divorce.

No more cocaine, but large amounts of alcohol and a lot of time spent at the bar, desperately trying to find someone to love me. One abusive relationship after another — black eyes, split lips, broken nose, giant nasty black and blue marks all over my body, repeatedly being strangled into unconsciousness, the back of my head split wide open. One more failed marriage. No self-respect. No self-esteem. No sense of self-worth. My children bounce back and forth between me and their dads—my situations never seem to be stable enough for them to be safe with me for any length of time. Three surgeries on my face to (somewhat) correct the damage caused by being punched on the left side of my jaw too many times.

One more angry and abusive relationship—this is what I know. This is where I'm comfortable. This is "normal" for me. I hate my life, but this is my life, isn't it? I often wonder why it has to be this way—but this is the way it is, and I have resigned myself to it.

I desperately want to be loved, but I know now that it's never going to happen. I have no clue what the point of my life might be. Why did I ever have to be born?

That is the first thirty-four years of my life in a nutshell. I was a person who never really learned how to dream, or "think big," because I never, ever believed that I could be anything different from the victim that I knew myself to be. Even when my dreams did come true (for example, my children), I couldn't allow myself to see them as "dreams come true" because my paradigm had me convinced that I didn't deserve to have any happiness for myself. So I didn't have any lasting happiness even though I did experience the joy of having my children. I know, it's a contradiction and it doesn't make sense to someone who hasn't lived it. But if you *have* lived it, then you know exactly what I'm talking about.

If this resembles—in any way—your life right now, then please continue reading. If you feel stuck in a pattern that feels impossible to change—whether it be mild or severe, and no matter what aspect of your life it involves (health, finances, career, relationships, etc.) — know this: It doesn't have to stay that way. You CAN break those patterns and change your life!

Chapter 2

The Life and Times of a Paradigm

"To ignore the power of paradigms to influence your judgment is to put yourself at significant risk when exploring the future. To be able to shape your future you have to be ready and able to change your paradigm."
~ Joel Barker

In the previous chapter you witnessed the birth and growth of a paradigm in me that had me convinced that I was a piece of crap that would never amount to anything.

The paradigm was the "program" that I operated my whole life from. It was the lens that I saw my world through. As I looked at myself and the world from the paradigm's point of view, I saw pain and ugliness. I saw a world in which I would never be loved or happy because I just knew I didn't deserve either of those things.

You may have noticed that as I got older *I was reinforcing my own programming* with the thoughts that I was thinking. I was feeding the tyrant. With each limiting thought that was in agreement with the paradigm, the tyrant was strengthened. With each self-sabotaging choice I made, the tyrant grew more powerful and became more deeply entrenched.

Something that really needs to be made clear here: It is super easy to see how and when my paradigms (at least the more obvious ones) were created and reinforced. But you do not have to be a victim of child abuse or domestic violence to have paradigms. Every person on this planet has paradigms. You may have experienced the most joyful and healthy childhood imaginable, but you still have both positive and negative paradigms.

You could have accepted a core belief at the age of six that said, "Reading is difficult for me." And guess what your experience of reading would be. So any time you would try to improve your reading skills, that particular paradigm—which had been comfortably lying dormant as long as you weren't thinking of changing—would kick in, and the disparaging self-talk would begin. *"You don't actually think you're going to be able to do this, do you? Who do you think you are? You've never been able to read before—what makes you think you're going to be able to do it now?"* and on and on and on, until you felt so bad that you would have to give up just to get some relief.

Yes, we all have our individual paradigms. Some of the more common ones, which you can clearly see in anyone (except, of course, yourself), are:

- "I can't lose weight because slow metabolism runs in my family."
- "Nothing really good can happen for me without something happening to taint it and make it not so good."
- "All the good ones are taken."
- "I am accident-prone."
- "There's not enough for everyone."
- "If you have lots of money that means you're an asshole."

- "I am a slow learner."
- "I can't do math."
- "The only way to be secure is to have a full-time job."
- "It's not okay to get paid for doing what you love."

These are all limiting beliefs that I have just recently witnessed in people that I know personally. (Okay, the "slow metabolism" one is mine. The second one belongs to me, too. But neither of them will be with me much longer because I have finally recognized them, and I know what to look for now. The rest I have seen in others.)

That last one is really interesting because it often shows itself like this, "If I were to get paid to [dance] [paint] [write] [sky dive] [ride my bicycle] [insert what you love to do here] _____, it would lose its appeal to me and I wouldn't love doing it anymore." Isn't that interesting? The paradigm will use sly little ploys just like that. Those ploys will seem reasonable to the person living it, while at the same time making no sense at all to a person who does not have the same, or similar, kinds of paradigms.

Start paying attention to the language that people use, and the choices that they make, and you will see either the "tyrant" (also known as Fear) or the "loving and supportive friend" (also known as the "still small voice" or the "Voice for Love" or the "Voice for Truth") often. Begin to notice those things in yourself, too, and see if you can spot either of them at work. Take a look at your results — at what you're living right now — and you will begin to know what to look for in your language and your actions (or your lack of action, whichever the case may be). The more familiar you are with your thought processes, the better able you will be to take control of them when the paradigm tries to take over and keep you small.

And know, also, that there are societal, religious, cultural and national paradigms, too, the subject of which could be a whole book in itself. This is my own personal belief with regard to that: As *individuals* take their power back from their own personal tyrants, the paradigms of "mass consciousness" will automatically shift. For this reason, I don't see any real cause to do more than just make mention of them. If you are curious as to what some "mass consciousness" paradigms might be, try watching the news or talking with a friend, co-worker, or church member with the intention of recognizing those paradigms when they present themselves. Or listen to your own thoughts with that intention. Here are just a few things that you may hear:

- "The world is a dangerous place."
- "There's not enough for everyone."
- "You can't make a good living if you are uneducated."
- "Times are hard."
- "There are no jobs to be had."
- "People are bad and we need to spend lots of time, money, and effort in an attempt to protect ourselves and our children from them."

And the list goes on. These are just beliefs that have been ingrained in us. They get passed on from generation to generation because people have accepted them as "just the way it is," and we have to teach our children about "the way it really is," don't we? As a result of this, each generation grows up looking at the world with the expectation of seeing these things that have been learned from the previous generation, so these things are, of course, what we see. And we meekly accept them as truth because, well, they just *are,* aren't they? And since they just *are,* why would we make any effort to see them as anything different?

As you read this book you will see that *the world changes when we change the way we look at the world!* You will see this through the eyes and thoughts of a woman who was fully a victim for most of her life, until one day she turned on her television and made the discovery that she could change the patterns of her life by changing the patterns of her thought. She could change the world she lived in by choosing to see it differently.

Anyone can do this very thing—all it takes is the decision to do so, and then determined self-discipline. All it takes is the will, and the willingness, to *Pop Your Paradigm!*

So, what is "Popping your paradigm" and how does it work?

Imagine that your "tyrant" paradigm is a giant inflatable thumb, which hangs out above you all the time. (I love this image—it makes me laugh, which serves to begin easing the pressure off the second I remember it.) It's just happily hanging out there, satisfied, knowing that it is in control because it's so big and powerful. It's got some pressure on you just by virtue of it being there, but you are not feeling any discomfort because you're used to it. It's just *there,* showing itself as the "facts of your life." It just *is what it is,* and you can't change *what-is,* right? Most people don't bother trying to change *what-is,* because it's just too uncomfortable.

Why is it so uncomfortable? Allow me to explain.

One day you decide to do something different. You decide to actually go after something that you want. It's something that you really want, but you've never dared to do anything but daydream about it until now.

Now, though, you've made a solid and determined decision to go for it.

The tyrant perks up and starts paying attention — you will hear it in the back of your mind. The tyrant will have you whispering things like this to yourself: "I'd really love to do that, but I just don't know if I can. I don't have the education. I don't have the time. I can't afford it. I might be too old. I'm definitely too tall. My car is the wrong color. My teeth are too crooked. What if people think I'm weird?" You will begin hearing in your mind all the reasons why you either can't, or shouldn't, go for what you want. And all these little comments (even though they are complete nonsense) will seem perfectly reasonable to you. Now, this self-talk is a little uncomfortable, but not too bad so far, and if what you say you want is something that is either not really all that important to you, or you feel it is so far out of reach that you shouldn't bother trying, you'll let go of it right here and the tyrant will be happy. It will settle itself back down into satisfied control, a hidden program running in the background of your thoughts — that giant thumb hanging out in readiness just above you — keeping you stuck right where you are. You'll go back to living the same day, the same month, the same year, over and over again.

However... if you do not allow this little discomfort to stop you — oh boy, are you in for it!

The tyrant will be okay with you daydreaming, but the second you decide to take some real steps to change your life, guess what happens. WHAM!!! You are FLATTENED beneath that giant thumb! The tyrant does *not* want you thinking for yourself, or moving outside the parameters of the box that it thinks you belong in.

The instant you start to do any of that, the pressure is on—it seems to come out of nowhere—and it does not let up until you give up! That pressure will go from discomfort, to pain, to feeling suffocated, to feeling hopeless and powerless... until you finally feel forced to decide that it's not possible for you to have what you want. You decide that your Dream is really not worth the agony of feeling this way, and as you come to this conclusion, the tyrant knows that it has accomplished what it set out to do. It feels safe again, and so it releases the pressure. And you go back to your life inside the box, where you are comfortable.

But this will only happen if you do *not* recognize that it's really the paradigm frantically trying to keep you from changing. If you can recognize that it's just the tyrant trying to save its own life by using whatever means necessary to keep you where you are, then you are truly on your way to being in control of your own life. For the paradigm, it is a matter of its own life or death to keep you where you are, which will keep that tyrant safe and satisfied. If you change, grow, and move forward in your life, the tyrant thinks it will die, and so it does everything it can to terrify you into staying where you are.

As you read the rest of this book you will see example after example of what this looks like. Pressure. Pressure. Pressure. And how do you relieve this incredible pressure? You *Pop Your Paradigm,* of course!

I recently learned, from the Teacher previously mentioned—whom you will meet in the next chapter, and whom you will get to know fairly well (through my use of the principles that she teaches) as you progress through this story—about a concept that she calls the "Sword of Truth."

This is my understanding of her teaching, and THIS is what you use to pop that giant inflatable thumb, which is full of nothing more than hot air and bluster, that is the tyrant. A very important thing to remember about paradigms is this—they have no real substance. They have no power other than that which we give to them. The only really powerful thing a paradigm does is this: It makes the things that frighten us *seem* gigantic and very, very real. The paradigm is a master illusionist.

As I stated at the beginning of this book, I did not learn what a paradigm was until September of 2008. The journey described in the remainder of this book began nine years before that, in September of 1999.

The main body of this writing was completed in the spring of 2008, several months before I learned about the nature of paradigms—what they are and how they work.

Then, in January of 2009 I heard my Teacher describe the Sword of Truth and I realized that it was through the use of this Sword all those years ago that I was able to completely transform my life, even though at that time I had never been introduced to the concepts of "paradigm" or "Sword of Truth."

A Sword of Truth is nothing more or less than a thought that cuts right through the nonsense of a paradigm. Throughout the rest of this story you will find that it was ONLY through deliberately using thoughts like this—every one of which can be considered a Sword of Truth—that I was able to change (save) my own life.

A Sword of Truth, or a "God Thought," is a thought that is so in tune with Infinite Intelligence that the tyrant cannot hold its own against it.

For example: Let's say I have a paradigm that says the only way to have an income is through a "real" job. And then I lose my job and, of course, I panic.

> *Oh, my God! Now what am I going to do? I have all these bills to pay and no way to do it! I'm going to lose everything I have! The economy is terrible right now. I know there are no jobs out there, which means that I'm not going to be able to find one for myself, which means that, yep, I'm going to lose everything! What am I going to do? It's hopeless. Why did this have to happen to me? How am I going to feed my family? How am I going to make my house payment? How am I going to keep the electricity on? I give up.*

This is an abbreviated version of the type of scenario that the tyrant is so very good at creating. I mean, I just lost my job five minutes ago and I've already given up any hope of this being anything other than the end of all good things in my life.

So I'll pull out my Sword of Truth and pop a hole in this paradigm. My Sword of Truth, my "God Thought," needs to be something that I KNOW is the Truth. The FACT is that I have just lost my job. This is just a fact, and facts only have power that I give to them. TRUTH on the other hand, has Power of its own. All I need to do is know that Truth is Truth and that no fact, condition, or circumstance, has any power whatsoever to alter the Truth.

The fact is that the company I work for has found it necessary to let me go. What's the Truth? Wow. There are all sorts of Truths I could use here.

Here are just a few:

- The Truth is that a "real job" does not have to be my only source of income. There are an infinite number of ways that money can show up in my life.

- The Truth is that this just happened five minutes ago. Something could happen within the company and they could call me tomorrow and ask me to come back.
- The Truth is that the career I *really* want could be somehow opening up right now and that opportunity could, this very moment, be sitting in my e-mail inbox at home.
- The Truth is that my world is not ending right now. My bills are paid up to this point, so I do have room to breathe. It is not necessary for me to call this "bad" at this particular moment in time. I can if I choose to, but I don't have to.

I could go on and on with this, but I'm sure you get the picture. Every one of these statements, each in its own way, deflated and neutralized the paradigm. Each of these statements rendered the tyrant powerless and incapable of maintaining the pressure necessary to keep me trapped under its thumb.

Without a Sword of Truth, however, I would have continued to flail around in my panic. I would have continued frantically pushing against the tyrant, unknowingly feeding it with my fear. In my pushing against the problem I would have made the problem bigger and more powerful and I would have spiraled down to the condition that I had created initially *only in my thoughts* within the first five minutes of losing my job.

In using the Sword of Truth, though, I was able to see alternative after alternative, which meant that when a solution to my problem showed up (and there are ***always*** an infinite number of solutions available to me if I am willing to see them) I would have been open, willing, *and able,* to see that solution.

In allowing the facts to just be the facts, and placing my attention on the power to be found in the Truth, I was able to pop that paradigm and neutralize the programming right on the spot. And this left me free to try things that I never would have thought of attempting before. And, very likely (as with my own true story told in the remainder of this book), at the other end of the journey I would find myself profoundly grateful that the "problem" happened in the first place!

The previous example was about changing the "default" programming that kicks in when something we perceive as "bad" happens in our life as it is. But what about the one that kicks in when we decide we want to make our life better in some way?

That is what the remainder of this book is about. It's about my decision that I wanted to be safe in my own life, and my paradigm that said, "You don't deserve that. It'll never happen."

What's your Dream? Do you want to make a million dollars? Do you want to release fifty pounds from your body? Do you want to release an addiction? Do you want to travel the world and get paid to do it? Do you want to learn to fly a plane? What's stopping you? I guarantee that it's nothing outside of you that's keeping you from having what you want. It's the tyrant. It's the pressure of that giant thumb keeping you right where you are.

What you will experience in the rest of this book is an example of what it takes to break free of that thumb — to neutralize it and to become powerful in your own life.

I thought about going through the completed manuscript and pointing out all the places in which the tyrant showed up (WHAM!!!) and tried to suppress me and keep me from growing. And then I was going to point out the "loving and supportive friend," also, along with the various Swords of Truth that I used to pop holes in that giant thumb. And then I was going to explain how using each particular Sword helped me to be open to the next idea or opportunity that I could use to bring myself closer to the woman I wanted to become and the life I wanted to live. And I was also going to explain in each situation how, if I hadn't used each particular Sword, I would never have been able to see those ideas or opportunities (just because I would not have been looking for them), and my life would have turned out very differently.

But I have decided not to do all that, thank God! I think it will be much more meaningful for you to be deliberately looking for those things as you read of my adventures in learning how powerful my habits of thought really are. So, rather than just reading the story, it will be a little bit like you're actually participating. *If you will read the story with the intention of DELIBERATELY NOTICING the things described in the previous paragraph, you will get a much better idea of how this stuff works and how you can apply the principles that I learned from my Teacher in your own life to make it what you want it to be.*

I'm tossing you this opportunity to actually participate in the story and learn from it, instead of just reading it and thinking it's interesting but not applicable to your own life.

In my story the tyrant is easy to see, and so is the loving and supportive friend. As you go through this adventure with me, see if you can spot the various Swords of Truth that I used over and over again to deflate that giant thumb. And as you spot them, know that *you can do the same thing!* You really can change your life by neutralizing your programming. Have fun!

I'm going to start you off with one Sword of Truth, so you have an idea of what you're looking for as you progress through this story. This is the first thought of Truth that I ever deliberately used to change my perception of what I was experiencing. It is very subtle, and if I did not NOW recognize just how powerful it was THEN, I don't know that I would really call it a Sword of Truth. But in looking back, I see that—subtle as it is—it definitely qualifies, so I'm going to give it to you.

In August of 1999 I had a thought that I'd never *really* considered before. That thought was, "There's got to be a better way. There's got to be a better way for me to live than this!" Now, this thought had bounced across my mind many times before. The difference between those times and this time was that this time there was a part of me that was willing to believe it. My previous version of that thought was always something like this, *"I wish* there was another way for me to live." Or maybe, *"If only* there was another way for me to live." Do you see the difference? Unspoken, but strongly implied, were three additional words – *"but there isn't."* So it would have looked like this, "I wish there was another way for me to live, but there isn't." Or, "If only there was another way for me to live, but there isn't."

And then the thought wandered into my mind and stuck, "There's got to be a better way for me to live than this." Without this thought, and a willingness to believe it, none of the events in this book would have happened the way that they did. If I hadn't been able to believe this thought (even the tiniest little bit), when I found my Teacher on TV the following month, I would have said, "Baloney," when I heard what she had to say. Okay, that's not exactly the word I would have used, but I'm sure you get the idea. At any rate, I would have changed the channel and I would have continued to live under the thumb of the tyrant until I died, which would have been sooner rather than later.

Throughout this manuscript I mention over and over again that my Teacher and her work saved my life. Since this manuscript was completed I have come to a more accurate believing than that. What I've come to know—and finally give myself credit for—is this: Her Teaching had a profound effect on my life, yes, but it was *my willingness to put to use* the things that she taught that actually caused my life to change. She did not—she could not—do it for me. I had to take the steps myself.

At one point in the manuscript, I actually came close to saying it this way, but I wanted to say it here and now, because I want you to keep it in mind as you read the story.

Without my first Sword of Truth that said, "There's got to be a better way for me to live than this," which I remember saying to myself often during the weeks leading up to that fateful day in September, I would not have heard a word that my Teacher said when I found her on TV.

And without a willingness to take the things she said and *apply them* in my own life, I would have died young at the hands of another.

You will be introduced to my Teacher in the following pages, and if anything I've said about her and her Teaching feels big to you (in an, "Oh my God I can use this!!" kind of way), I cannot recommend highly or strongly enough that you find yourself some of her material, study it for yourself, and then *use* the principles that she teaches to powerfully and profoundly change your life.

And now… onward into the Journey!

Chapter 3

The Adventure Begins

"Let your hopes, not your hurts, shape your future."
~ Robert Schuller

In the beginning, there was my constant companion — the void. Okay, so it wasn't *really* a void, but it sure felt like a never-ending emptiness to me at the time.

It was September 19, 1999 and I was living in Portland, Oregon where I had spent most of my thirty-four years. I was involved with *another* abusive, angry man in a long line of abusive, angry men. This particular man did not allow me to see my children, who were sixteen and eleven at that time. He had not allowed me to spend any time with them for about a year and a half at this point in the relationship. If I wanted to see them I had to do it behind his back and, of course, I almost always got caught, which just proved to him how untrustworthy I was. After all, if I would sneak around to see my kids, what else was I doing when he wasn't there to watch me? Huh? Who was I talking to? What was I saying to people? Who was I having sex with? Never mind that I was working full time and going to school full time (because he *told* me to go to school!), and when I wasn't at work or at school I was in his presence. How come I got such good grades in school? It was because I was providing the entertainment in my classes, wasn't it? No, I wasn't just sleeping with my instructors to get good grades—I was "entertaining" the entire class, wasn't I?

Never mind that I spent every free moment I had on my homework. In his mind, the only reason I spent time on my homework was so I could avoid spending time with *him*. This man actually believed this stuff, and no matter what I did to try to prove to him that I wasn't the horrible, awful person that he constantly made me out to be, it was never enough. In fact, the things I did to try to prove that I was a good person usually backfired right in my face and made things worse. I was miserably unhappy. But he said that he loved me, and I so very desperately wanted to be loved…

It's Sunday afternoon, September 19, 1999 and I am alone in the apartment. Jeff is outside washing his truck. I am flipping through the channels looking for something to watch on TV. Nothing on the "good" channels appeals to me. I land on Oregon Public Broadcasting (OPB). There's a blonde woman wearing a bright pink outfit standing on a platform in front of an audience. I hear her say, "We all—every one of us—deserve to have our dreams come true."

My thought is along these lines: *"Yeah, right. Whatever. My dreams will never come true."* I don't even know *how* to dream. What I'm feeling right now would be diagnosed as chronic depression if I were to go see a doctor. I do not believe the things this woman is saying because I have every aspect of my own life as proof that she is wrong. But she has so much energy, and she seems to really believe the stuff that she's talking about. I find that I can't get myself to change the channel. I have no idea who this woman is, but her enthusiasm has caught my attention and I feel as if I *need* to hear what she has to say. I keep listening.

A short time later, she says something that really catches my attention—it's something that I'm ready to hear, I guess. She is quoting Lao Tse, and what she says is this, "If you continue down the road you're on, you're going to end up where you're headed." I suck in my breath in shock as my body involuntarily bolts upright—these sixteen words have hit me like a bucket of water in my face.

My mind races frantically as I try to absorb what I have just heard: *If you continue down the road you're on, you're gonna end up where you're headed. Where am I headed? Where is the road I'm on taking me? Oh, my God! I don't want to go where I'm headed! If I stay on this road I'm going to DIE at the hands of a man who constantly and repeatedly tells me that he loves me! Or worse, I'm going to be crippled by him and then AT HIS MERCY for the rest of my life, for however long I might live.* **(Panic! Panic! Panic! Despair.** Sorrow. Intense pain. Resignation. Depression. Apathy…) *It is so sad that this is what I have to look forward to.*

If you continue down the road you're on, you're gonna end up where you're headed! But I've tried making u-turns! That doesn't work! I have left him six times in the last year and a half, and he always finds me and makes me come back. Or he threatens my kids so I feel like I have to come back. Or he harasses me at work until I feel I have no choice but to come back. And when

I do come back I get punished. U-turns don't work — leaving doesn't work! Leaving just makes things worse because he gets angrier and more violent every time. So I HAVE NO CHOICE but to stay on this road!

But if I stay on this road, I can see my destination very clearly. I'm either going to die at the hands of this man who says that he loves me, or he's going to put me in a wheelchair for the rest of my life. What can I do? I'm damned if I do and I'm damned if I don't. I'll die if I stay. I'll die if I leave. Why does my life have to be this way? Why do I even bother trying?

As these thoughts run through my head in a matter of seconds, the blonde woman on television keeps talking. I continue to listen.

She says, "If you continue down the road you're on, you're going to end up where you're headed." And then she goes on to say that if you don't like the road you're on, you can change direction. *(Yeah, right! Whatever.)* All you have to do is make a *little* shift in direction—ten degrees, one degree, or even just a fraction of a degree—and a mile down the road, you're in a whole new place. *(Oh, my God! I might be able to do that!)* As she talks about this, she places her hands together in front of her, fingers pointing straight out ahead of her. Then, as she says the words "little shift in direction" she angles her right hand out away from her left hand. Then she moves both hands forward, the left one in the original direction it had been pointing, and the right one out at an angle. As she does this she says, "A mile down the road, you're in a whole new place." I can actually *SEE* what she means. That visual is burned into my brain…a little shift in direction and a mile down the road I can be in a whole new place. Is this really possible for me?

The program I'm watching continues for about another hour and a half and everything this woman says touches a place inside of me that I had never known was there. I don't know what this place is at the time—but I will soon discover it. Later, as I think and wonder about it, I find that the name of this place is Hope. This is a wonderful, powerful, awesome place to discover inside your self!

As OPB takes its fundraising breaks, I discover that the blonde woman is a minister. (This discovery almost has me changing the channel immediately, because I do not believe in God. In fact, just the thought of God usually makes me gag and get angry.) Her name is Mary Manin Morrissey and the program is called *Building Your Dreams,* and it's based on a book that she has written called *Building Your Field of Dreams.* OPB is offering a video of the program and a copy of the book for a pledge of "just" $120.00. Well, that seems like a lot of money if you don't have it. But I am convinced that this book can change my life. This is an incredible feeling that I have—it is so powerful! I struggle with this feeling throughout the show. The more I watch, the more convinced I become that my life depends upon getting a copy of that book and video.

*But how can I do that? There is no way in hell that Jeff will allow me to pledge $120 to OPB. In fact, I don't think he would ever let me buy a book like that at all. But they keep saying I can pay for it over the course of a year – just $10 a month. Besides, it's **MY** checking* *account, isn't it? If I commit to it, he won't be able to do anything about it. All I have to do is make sure that the $10 is there every month. I can do that, can't I?*

He comes in for a drink of water, pays no attention to what I'm watching, goes back outside to his truck.

Okay, he was just in here, so it'll probably be a while before he comes back in. Will I have time to make the call and not get caught? I am scared to death! If he comes in and catches me on the phone I'm going to get hurt. But this is so important — I feel like my life depends on whether or not I can get myself to pick up the phone. I wish I could see the driveway from here, so I'll know if he heads back inside, but I can't. Am I going to let that stop me? I am petrified, but I reach for the phone. *Nope, I can't get myself to pick it up. What if he comes in and catches me? I can't do it.*

One of the things that Mary speaks about in the program is fear. (She says as part of her presentation, "I see you, Fear. I know you're there. You have no power over me.") What I'm feeling right now is way beyond fear. It's more along the lines of terror. I feel as if I'm having a heart attack. My heart is trying to pound its way out of my chest. My hair is standing on end. My ears are ringing. I can feel my eyes bulging, as if my eyeballs are trying to pop out of their sockets. My hands are slick with sweat. *If he catches me on the phone he will hurt me. But this is so important! What should I do?*

As Mary talks about fear she quotes William Shakespeare:

"*Our doubts are traitors, and make us lose the good we oft might win — by fearing to attempt.*"

This gets my attention in a very big way: *What is the good that I will lose if I am too afraid to even try? What will I have if I **don't** try? Am I willing to let my fear have control? Am I willing to keep doing what I've been doing? What is the bigger fear? Am I more afraid of him catching me on the phone and punishing me right now? Or is the bigger fear that of living the rest of my life scared to death of this man who says that he loves me?*

That decides it for me. I pick up the phone. My heart is still pounding. It feels like it's going to burst. My ears are still ringing. My hands are still slippery. I'm in a state of hyper-awareness—seeing, hearing, feeling everything in sharp, minute detail. This is what absolute terror feels like. I don't like it! I keep in mind what my life will be like from now until forever if I can't get past my "fear to attempt." I dial the number. It rings on the other end. A woman answers. It seems to take an *eternity* for my order to be placed. The entire time I'm on the phone, I am gripped by thoughts of the pain he could cause me. *What if he catches me? What if he catches me? What do I think I'm doing? What do I think I'm doing? Just what the hell do I think I'm doing?! Oh my God! Oh my God! Oh my God!*

After what feels like a year on the phone—during which he could walk in the front door at any time—my order has been placed. *(Okay, it's all right to breathe now...)* Now I just have to wait six to eight weeks for my book and my video to arrive. I can't believe that I've done it. I can't believe I've done something like this *without his permission!* I still feel as if my heart might explode, but now my sense of self-respect has just shot through the roof.

I am amazed at how wonderful I feel right now, in spite of the fact that I'm scared to death and I have no idea how I'm going to explain things when my merchandise arrives. Maybe I really do have a backbone?

Oh yeah, he'll probably push the redial button on the phone when he comes in. He knows that the last call I made was to the bank to see what's happened in my checking account since yesterday. I'd better get that number back into the phone or he'll know that I've done something I wasn't supposed to do.

That phone call was my first step onto the road that has led me to where I am today.

I ordered *Building Your Field of Dreams* on that day in September of 1999 and I received it about five weeks later, at the end of October.

During those five weeks I practiced "shifting my direction." I decided to start with something that seemed to be small, but turned out to be huge. I decided not to cry anymore when Jeff called me a slut or accused me of sleeping around. I decided that I didn't have to react to that at all. This was much easier to say than it was to actually do. In fact, most of the time — at first, anyway — I would forget until it was too late. But in those times when I did remember, I could feel myself taking some of my power back from him. I was tired of him deliberately making me feel small and worthless, and after watching *Building Your Dreams* and soaking up those principles like a sponge, I decided to consciously *use* some of the stuff I had learned from that program. I decided I didn't have to allow him the power to push that particular button and get the reactions that he depended on to make himself feel superior. I made a concerted effort to break that button. This was a very simple thing to do, but it sure wasn't easy! It didn't always work because I had thirty-four years of conditioning and habit to get past. But I made a conscious effort to break that conditioning and those habits and see his petty little manipulations for what they actually were, which were just attempts to control me, because he was unable to control himself. He desperately needed to be in control of *something,* and I had cooperated so willingly with that need for the previous eighteen months. When I remembered to look at his behavior — and my cooperation with his behavior — in that light, it became easier and easier to break my own patterns of victim consciousness that had been all I had known throughout my life up to this point. In breaking those patterns, I was short-circuiting the buttons that had always worked so well for him to get the reactions from me that he *needed* me to provide for him, so that he could feel powerful and in control. (I was not the only one in this relationship whose behavior was dictated by subconscious programming.)

Looking back to that point in my relationship with him, I can see that breaking my buttons was probably not the smartest thing for me to do. Domestic violence is about power and control, and if the abuser feels that power and control slipping away, the violence almost always escalates. And yes, things did get worse — but I *felt* better. I felt strong. It was an incredible feeling to know that I did not *have* to react the way he wanted (or needed) me to. It was an amazing experience to break that habit of reaction and to know that I didn't have to cooperate in whatever ugliness he tried to create. As a result of making that one decision to shift my direction I could feel myself growing. I could feel a tiny little flame inside my soul ignite, and the more I made the choice not to react to his pettiness and his need to make me feel bad, the steadier that flame became. It really does take two to fight, and if one of the two refuses to engage, then the one left eventually runs out of the fuel needed to sustain the fight. In the case of domestic violence this usually leads to an explosion on the part of the abuser, and physical pain for the victim. I feel fortunate to still be alive, but I have absolutely no doubt that it was an experience that was right for me to go through, because during that experience I found a deep knowing in myself that I *am* powerful and that I don't have to hand my power over to any person or circumstance, no matter how much pain that person or circumstance is causing me. That experience was appropriate for me, and it was exactly what I needed to prove to myself that it was possible for me to shift my direction and take steps toward what I actually wanted in my life. I could create my own road, rather than be dragged unwillingly down his. September 19, 1999 was the day my whole life changed…

So I practiced that one little (huge) thing while I waited for my book to arrive. I received it at the end of October, 1999. Jeff's lack of reaction when I received my package amazes me to this day. He barely even asked me about it. He thought the $10 a month was funny and he thought that trying to keep me from having it when I needed to pay it was funny. He thought that paying $120 for a book and a video was funny. Little did he know that the book and the video were worth far more than a piddly little $120 to me. They were worth my life, which is precious, and priceless! There is not even the tiniest shred of doubt in my mind that *Building Your Field of Dreams* absolutely saved my life. When I received that book, I read it straight through, to the exclusion of just about everything else. All I can say is that I must have been ready to find out who I really was, because in that book I found out who I really am.

Before I go any further with this, I guess I'd better explain why what I found in Mary's book is such a big deal to me — why what I found in her book was just plain *profound* to me.

I feel very fortunate that Mary only said the "G" word once or twice during the program, because if she had said it any more than that I would have changed the channel out of pure irritation. I don't know that I had ever in my life really believed in God — I had never had a reason to. The sexual abuse from a "Saved" person who hid behind Jesus was the beginning of my disillusionment as a very young child. And then my South Carolina foster home experience was proof enough for me as a nine-year-old that if God did exist, He certainly didn't love *me*. In fact, from age nine on through my teenage years and my adulthood I had always just "known" that, if there really was a God, He surely hated me. There was never any question of that in my mind — God hated me, and I hated God. Over the years I gradually discovered that it was a lot easier not to believe in God at all than it was to hate Him, so that was what I did — at least until someone said the "G" word in my presence. Then I would get angry and that hatred would surface again.

I think it is no coincidence that in the month of August of 1999, I came to the conclusion that I needed something more in my life. It was obvious that my life was not working out well for me the way it was. I had recently begun thinking, "There's got to be a better way to do this. There's just got to be a better way!" That August I shocked myself with a decision to visit a Baptist church that was about a mile from my apartment. Do you have any idea how hard it is to walk into a church when just the thought of religion makes you want to throw up? When I say I shocked myself with that decision, I am not exaggerating even a little bit.

My goodness, Jeff got upset when I said I wanted to check out that church. He was upset that I felt the need for something more in my life. He was upset that I was feeling a need to grow, to stretch out the sides of the box I lived in with him. He said that wasn't *me*, and that he didn't know who I was becoming to want something deeper in my life than what I already had. After all, what I had was pretty good, wasn't it? Well, yeah, it was pretty good if I could ignore the fact that it felt like he was threatening my life every time he said to me, "It's you and me forever, baby." What I had was pretty good if I could ignore the fact that I wasn't allowed to be any kind of a mother to my children. My life was pretty good if I could just ignore the fact that I had to take my panties down for him whenever he wanted me to—no matter what I was doing and whether I wanted to or not—because if I didn't, he would make damn sure I regretted it. My life was great if I could just ignore the fact that I wasn't allowed to have any contact with anyone in my life who loved me or cared about me in any way. My life was wonderful if I could just get past the fact that I was desperately, desperately unhappy.

He didn't tell me that I couldn't go to church, which surprised me until I found out later that he would use it as a reason to pick fights with me.

I only went three times. The first time was okay. I met people who seemed nice and the service was all right as long as I suppressed the irritation that I felt about all that "Jesus is my Savior, but I'll never get to Heaven because I'm so bad" stuff. The second time I went was okay, too, and I became a little more comfortable with the idea of stepping foot inside a church. The third time was the charm, though. The last time I went into that building convinced me that I didn't ever want to set foot in a church again and that I had made a mistake to even consider going in the first place. That particular service was incredibly distasteful to me and by the time it was over I was even more convinced than I had been for most of my life that Christians were nothing but a bunch of hypocrites and that I really wanted nothing to do with them.

Yes, I know, that was very judgmental of me, but I couldn't control it—and I saw no reason to try. You see, I had always *heard* that Christian people were supposed to be so loving and kind and generous and all that blah blah blah. My experiences throughout my life, however, had taught me that Christian's were mean and judgmental people who only loved others on Sunday, in the church building, during the service. My experiences with Christian people had been that they thought it was okay for them to "sin" because they had already been "saved" by Jesus. And because they had been "saved" and I hadn't, they felt justified in looking down their noses at me and calling me "sinner." Throughout my life the Christian religions had taught me that God was a mean-spirited old man with a long white beard up in the sky who was looking down on me and judging everything I did. I had learned that, no matter how good I tried to be, I would never get into Heaven if I didn't accept Jesus as my Savior. And that once I accepted Jesus as my Savior I could do any mean, hurtful, or just plain *wrong* thing I wanted because I had already been forgiven. I wanted nothing to do with a God like that—that God seemed hypocritical, contradictory, and untrustworthy. That belief just didn't feel right to me, basically because some of the most hurtful things that had ever been done to me had been done by those "God-fearing Christians" that were so willing to condemn others who didn't believe what they believed. For most of my life I had said, "No thanks, I'd rather go to Hell than believe it's okay to hurt people because they don't believe what I believe."

And then at the age of thirty-four I decided I needed something more in my life. I didn't know what that "more" was, but I was willing to see if I could maybe, possibly find "it" in the church closest to my home. And as I said previously, the first two times I went were okay and I was able to suppress my irritation and concede that maybe I had some prejudices of my own that I needed to let go of. After all, just because the religious people that I knew personally had been hurtful, mean-spirited hypocrites didn't mean that *all* religious people were like that...

During the first week I decided that church hadn't been so bad and that just because I hadn't instantly found what I was looking for that day didn't mean that I wouldn't come across it the following Sunday. So I went again, and had the same kind of thoughts again. The third time I was proved right about "those people." I was so upset by what was taught that day—I couldn't help but feel sad for the sheep in that congregation who sat there and blindly said "hallelujah" and "amen" throughout that service. That "God-fearing," "loving" "man of God" stood up in front of the congregation that day and taught that God says that white people are supposed to stay separate from, and look down on, black people. I am not kidding and I am not exaggerating! I wish I could remember the passages from the bible that he quoted (twisted, warped). I do remember that he talked about an African-American basketball player having his hands around his white coach's throat and lots of African-American people thinking that it was okay to excuse him for doing that because of skin color. (If you remember that particular incident, then I'm sure you know the names of the people involved. If not, then please just take it for what it is, which is history—just something that happened, and I'd rather leave it as impersonal as I can.) That incident was this minister's "proof" that whites should stay separate from (and above) blacks. I, myself, having been abused by numerous people in my life (and all of them were white, including the one who used to put his hands around my throat and strangle me into unconsciousness), am of the opinion that doing things that hurt other people is wrong. Plain and simple; black, white, red, green, or purple! It's not okay to hurt somebody just because they are different from you or you are different from them.

When I was forced to go to church as a child, there was a song that we sang that went like this: "Red and yellow, black or white. All are precious in His sight. Jesus loves the little children of the world." Maybe those Baptists at that church didn't know that song. I don't know. What I do know is that I left that church that day feeling more than ever like religion wasn't for me and that if I had to believe that being prejudiced against someone because of the color of their skin (or mine) was the way to get God to love me and let me into Heaven, I'd rather go to Hell.

Okay, so I knew I needed something more, but obviously Christianity wasn't it. I didn't have the stomach for it. If you, the reader, are a Christian (or a black, white, green or purple person) and you choose to be offended by the things I've said here, well that is your choice and please feel free to judge me by these few paragraphs if it feels right for you to do so. Or you can take it for what it is, which is how I felt *at that time.*

And then, about four Sundays after my last visit to a church, I heard a lady named Mary Manin Morrissey say, "If you continue down the road you're on, you're going to end up where you're headed." I heard her talk about "co-creation" and dreams and joy. I heard her talk about getting past Fear. I heard her talk about learning to look at "problems" in a different way and from a different level. I heard her talk about these things and I was present to every single thing she said. I was open and willing to actually *hear* her. She did say the "G" word, but I was able to get past that and not change the channel in a huff because I actually *heard* her when she said, "Don't let the *word* [God] get in your way of understanding what I'm saying."

I've heard it said that when the student is ready, the teacher will appear. I was ready. I was ready to discover a new way to live my life. I was ready to learn that my happiness depended on only one person, and that person was me. I was ready to learn that I had strength that I never would have guessed was a part of me. I was ready to learn that it was all right for me to have dreams and actually expect them to come true. I was ready to accept that I did not have to keep surviving the same life over and over again. I was ready to start breaking some of the patterns that were a part of my personal belief system. I was ready to end my life as "victim." I was ready to change my way of looking at things and I was ready to start making different choices for myself. I was ready to learn how to be happy.

I was thirty-four years old and I don't think I had ever felt so alive or had so much hope for my future as I did during those ninety minutes of listening to that tiny little blonde woman who had so much positive energy to share with anyone willing to accept it from her.

During the following weeks, while I was waiting for my book to arrive, I consciously and deliberately held onto the things I had heard her say during that hour-and-a-half that changed my life so profoundly. When Jeff would be a jerk to me and do things to hurt me on purpose, I tried not to fall in with him. I tried to remember that just because he felt a need to pour toxic energy into our relationship, I did not have to join him. I wasn't always successful, but the more I made an effort to remember, the sooner I would catch myself and the easier it was to stop myself from going there with him in the first place. I found that the more I practiced this, the more peaceful I felt. And the more peaceful I felt, the angrier he became. And the angrier he became, the easier it was for me to remember that I could make a life-affirming choice *for myself* instead of a "You are mean and I hate you" choice that was directed *at him.*

I did not realize until years later that, as I was going through this process, I was preparing myself to be ready to read *Building Your Field of Dreams* with an open mind, heart, and attitude.

My book arrived at the end of October 1999 and I jumped in with both feet.

I did not just *read* that book. I submerged in it. I immersed myself in it. And when I came up for air I found that I had changed.

Have you ever seen a sponge that has been separated from water for so long that it is hard, brittle, and shriveled to less than half of its full, "healthy" size? That hard, brittle sponge was me. I had so long been separated from any hope of ever having anything good happen in my life that I had become just like that dried out sponge. My spirit felt dry, brittle, empty—as if I had no life or substance to me. My soul felt like a shriveled up, unhealthy, dried out husk. My life was a black hole, a void, an empty vessel that was finally ready to be filled. I was so thirsty for what Mary had to say that I soaked every bit of it in, concept by concept and principle by principle. And when I was done I felt bigger and more alive than I had ever felt before.

As I jumped into *Building Your Field of Dreams*, I learned things that I never would have considered could be possible for me. During that experience I found out who I really am. As I soaked up what Mary had to say, I discovered a God I could believe in. I discovered a God that is not separate from me. I discovered that I am not just a Child of God, I am a *part* of God. In Mary's book I found a God of Love, Light, and Oneness with all things.

Did you know that the word "sin" is an archery term? It means "missing the mark." The God that Mary talks about in her book would never stop loving me or condemn me for *anything*, much less something as insignificant and unimportant as "missing the mark." I had always had difficulty with the concept of "original sin," and in Mary's book I found an idea that I could embrace that she calls "original innocence."

As I read that book I learned to look at "sin" and "original innocence" like this: People make mistakes—people "miss the mark." Have you ever shot a bow and arrow? I don't think that any person who ever picked up a bow and tried to shoot it hit what they were aiming at the very first time. In fact, the first thing they probably hit was the inside of their forearm with the bowstring. That's what I did, and guess what—it hurt! A lot! And I ended up with a huge bruise, but I didn't let that stop me. I "missed the mark" and caused myself some pain, but I didn't set the bow down and give up. I kept trying. I practiced taking aim and releasing the bowstring. And the more I practiced, the more "true" my aim was.

As I thought more and more about this—as I thought about all the times during my life that I had "missed the mark" (and there were *lots* of them!), as I remembered all the things I had done in my life that I felt bad about, that I was ashamed of, that I wished I hadn't done, that I continually beat myself up for—I came to the realization that I could let all that stuff go if I chose to. After all, it was all stuff that was in the past, right? It was all stuff that I could never change. I could feel bad and I could feel bad and I could feel bad, and no matter how bad I felt about my history it would never, ever change, would it? What would happen if I just worked at making healthier choices for myself starting right now? Wouldn't that go a long way toward shifting my direction? What if I just practiced aiming at what I *wanted* to experience in my life? What if I were to start aiming at what was in front of me, instead of continually looking behind me and wishing my life had been different? Hmmm...

One of the things that Mary had talked about in the TV program was something that Albert Einstein said. He said, "The most important question we can ever ask ourselves is this: Do I live in a friendly universe? Or do I live in a hostile universe?" How I look at my life is up to me. I can choose to see a friendly universe, or I can choose to see a universe that hates me. Up until this point in my life I hadn't known that I could make that kind of choice. Hearing Mary talk about it really gave me something to think about. What would happen if I made a deliberate choice to see the Universe as friendly? For years and years I had said to myself, "My life hates me." What if I made a concentrated effort to see just the opposite of that? Could changing my thinking really make that kind of difference in my life? Could looking at things in a different way really help me to see things differently? I decided I was willing to try it and see.

I began applying this "friendly universe" idea to my own life. I was tired of believing the lie that I was basically bad and that God was judging me and punishing me. I am a good person and I have always been a good person. Just because I have "missed the mark" sometimes doesn't mean that I am bad, and it doesn't mean that I must be punished for all eternity. All it means is that my aim wasn't True. It means that my aim was pulled off course by beliefs or attitudes that were not in alignment with my Good. Should I be punished for that? I think not. I think I should just keep consciously practicing until I connect with what I'm aiming for. And if I can do that with the belief that the Universe I live in is friendly, and that It wants me to have what I want, then that makes it that much easier to keep trying.

I have learned over the last few years that when I'm moving in the direction of my Dreams, if I do it with the attitude that the universe is hostile and against me, it is very easy to give up. It's easy to say, "I just knew it wasn't meant for me to have this dream." It's easy to set it down and not try anymore.

I have also learned over the last few years that when I'm moving in the direction of my Dreams, if I do it with the attitude that the universe is friendly and wants me to be happy, it is very easy to keep moving forward. I can always try again if I "miss the mark" or make a mistake. (Now there's a word... let's take a look at it. Mistake. Mis-take. How many "takes" does it take to make a movie? How many times do the actors have to do the same "take" over and over again before they get it right? Something to think about as we make mis-takes in our own lives, huh?) I can say, "Lesson learned. I'll try it a different way the next time."

I can tell you from experience—having tried it both ways—that choosing to see a friendly universe is much more fun than the other way around. Choosing to see a friendly universe moves you toward your Dreams, while seeing hostility will only move you farther away from the life you want.

This is just the barest tip of what I learned as I read *Building Your Field of Dreams.* In the following chapters you will see the unfoldment of a dream. Through these last several years, since I began deliberately using these principles, my life has become richer and richer and I have reached bigger and bigger Dreams.

The first in a long line of dreams was just to stay alive and learn how to really live, instead of merely existing or surviving. This did happen for me, in wonderful and profound ways. I don't believe it was a coincidence that Mary Morrissey and her teachings came into my life at the time and place that I was ready to receive them. There is also absolutely no question that I would not be alive today if Mary and her teachings had not come into my life when they did.

If I hadn't found her on television that day and really *listened* to the things she had to say, there is no doubt in my mind that I would have died at the hands of a man that I loved—a man who claimed to love me.

If I hadn't found her on TV that day, I would not now be living the life of my Dreams, and I would not now be setting the example for my children that Dreams can come true and patterns can be broken.

If I had continued to believe that the universe I lived in was hostile, I would have continued to experience a hostile universe.

If I had not learned for myself that patterns can be broken, I would have died at the bottom of the downward spiral that is formed in the "cycle of violence" that kills so many, many people every day.

If I had continued to believe that I was weak, I never would have found the strength to make the changes in my life that I needed to make to get me to the wonderful place I find myself in today.

And where do I find myself today? Today I am in a healthy, happy relationship, married to a man who is not afraid to love me and who encourages me to grow and become *more* of who I really am. Today I have written a workbook and created a workshop called SWAN, which is an acronym for Somebody Worth Accepting Now. SWAN is based on the tools that I used to get away—and stay away—specifically from my last abuser, but also from abusive situations and people in general. These tools are nothing less than the practical application of the principles that I learned from Mary Morrissey and *Building Your Field of Dreams.* Today this very powerful, very positive workshop has been presented in domestic violence shelters around the state of Arizona. Today I am an experienced speaker, and I have spoken regularly—to shelter staff, politicians, judges and attorneys, police officers, hospital staff, and prison inmates—over the last several years in the capacity of Survivor. Today I know how to catch rattlesnakes, and I ride a Harley. Today I am a published author, having written a book called *Choose Your Universe,* at the request of a couple of hundred prison inmates. Today—finally, and basically for the first time—I have good relationships with both of my children. And today, after years and years of hating my life and hating myself, I am able to love and accept myself for who I am, and I know that I deserve to have all the good in my life that I could ever dream of.

If I had continued down the road I was on, I would have ended up where I was headed. I am so very grateful that I didn't end up there, and that I learned that it was possible to make the shifts in my direction that were necessary to get me to *this* whole new place!

So what are some of the things that Mary said in *Building Your Field of Dreams* that made such a difference in my life? Here are just a few examples…

"Your history need not determine your destiny."

"…if you were starting fresh with a no-limits attitude, what would you do?"

"If you do what you've always done, you'll get the results you've always gotten."

"A dream cannot come true unless you dream that dream."
— Oscar Hammerstein —

"Living in limitation gradually squeezes the life out of you."

"She recognized that all along life had not been victimizing her. She'd been trapped by old ideas that limited her."

"Where I place my attention, I place my intention."

"When we say, "I'm trying," the truth is that we are participating at less than full commitment."

"The universe can do for you only what it can do through you."

"But we will not find the good if we keep our mind closed to it."

"No matter how wondrous the bequest, to the person with hands clenched, the gift remains unopened, unappreciated."

"Act as if you're worthless, and the universe will verify your belief."

"Limitation has no more power than my own belief in it." (Paraphrased)

"A third and essential way to help you feel more deserving of your dreams is by practicing gratitude… Gratitude forms a connecting link, a bridge between you and every possible channel of good in your life."

"Believe in your "original innocence." You make mistakes out of ignorance, not from a core of evil."

"I can choose peace instead of this."
— A Course in Miracles —

"Trust the process. If you are headed in a particular direction, confident of your purpose, you cannot help but bump into people proceeding along the same path."

These are just a few sentences taken from *Building Your Field of Dreams,* the book that literally saved my life. If you want to find out who you really are and what you really can do with your life, I recommend that you find yourself a copy of that book, sit down with it with an open mind and a no limits attitude, and pay attention to what happens within you. Your life will never be the same.

Now please join me for a look at how the principles I learned from Mary have radically and permanently turned my life around, just because I was willing to actually *apply* them in a practical way to change my experience of my life and my circumstances...

Chapter 4

Peace Begins With Me

"I can choose peace instead of this."
~ A Course in Miracles ~

I learned so many things during the nine months between the day I found Mary Morrissey on TV and the day I found it necessary to make the most important choice I've ever made in my life: That choice being, should I run for my very life? Or stay and die a violent, painful death at the hands of this man that I love? What do I want to be known as and remembered for? Do I want to be a Survivor? Or a statistic?

In order for me to even be able to ask myself these questions, I had to learn things that I had never considered possible before. In the process of deciding to look at the universe as friendly, I found that I had to change the way I looked at *everything* in my life. This is easy to talk about. It's not so easy to do... But it's not impossible, either. The fact that I am alive and *enjoying my life* today is proof that it can be done!

One of the things I learned was that it was perfectly all right for me to allow my dreams to be something more than just wishful thinking. Another was that peace begins with me. These were not the only things I learned during that period of time, but these two things — dreams and peace — were the foundation for the transformation of my entire life. If I had not learned these two basic things I have no doubt that I would be dead now, remembered as a statistic of domestic violence.

Do you believe that you can live your dreams? As I read Mary's book I became convinced that it was possible. I used *Building Your Field of Dreams* as if it were a "how-to" book because in it Mary provides very clear step-by-step instructions for growing your dreams. It is a great book for someone like I was back then. I was a person who really had no idea how to dream, but I was willing to learn. In that book I discovered how to plant the seed of a dream, how to weed out things that would choke the life out of my dream, how to nurture my dream and treat it with tender loving care. I learned how to have faith that my dream would grow even though I couldn't see it sprouting yet. I learned that it was okay to start with small dreams — to take baby steps — and work my way toward bigger ones, but that it's great to have big dreams, too. In fact, I've heard Mary say many times, "If you think you can do it on your own, without help from a Higher Power, then you're not dreaming big enough." You would think that only applies to the big ones, wouldn't you? Oh, no. When I first started learning how to dream I had to do it small because I had lived for so long just "knowing" that my dreams would never come true. I wasn't able to even consider dreaming big dreams. Let's put it this way, at that time my "little" dreams were enormous. Everything I wanted to accomplish felt like something I would need lots of help with.

I started out dreaming of peace in my relationship with Jeff. I didn't want to have to be afraid of him anymore. I loved him and I dreamed of a healthy relationship with him. I dreamed of growing a backbone and learning how to stand up for myself. I dreamed of him learning how to be happy with me. I dreamed of a relationship with him based on love, trust, and respect instead of fear, intimidation, suspicion, and resentment.

For nine months I worked toward these things and I grew as a person. During those nine months I practiced remembering to see the universe as friendly. I practiced looking for the good in every situation. I practiced looking for things to be grateful for. I practiced looking at everything from a place of knowing that I deserved a good life. I use the word "practice" here because, as with learning anything new, I wasn't very good at any of these things at first. I am, after all, a human being and I often completely forgot about the dreams I had decided on. And then I would get upset with myself for forgetting or for handling some situation in an "unskillful" manner. So then I'd have to remind myself that I lived in a friendly universe and that it had taken me thirty-five years to get where I was—I could, if I chose to, just forgive myself and move on. It was a learning process that I was going through. It was a learning process that I had to go through at that time in order for me to move forward in my life at all. And do you want to know something? It's been a lot of years and I still forget sometimes! I'm *still* practicing.

During those nine months of growth I left that man three more times before I finally had to run. Each of those three times, I grew that much stronger. And each time I went back it was more and more on my terms instead of just because I was afraid of what he would do to me or my children if I didn't come back, which had always been the case before.

During those nine months I had my dreams of a healthy relationship with him, but I also knew that he had to want to make it a good relationship, too. It takes two to fight, right? Well, it also takes two to make a relationship work.

We each wanted very different things. I wanted a peaceful, happy relationship. He wanted power over me and control of everything I did. I wanted to grow and I wanted him to grow with me. He wanted our lives to stay small. He was comfortable in his little box and he wanted me to stay in there with him. I wanted to be free to make my own choices, talk to people I wanted to talk to, wear what I wanted to wear, and go to the bathroom without his permission once in a while. He wanted me under his thumb.

So I had my dreams, and I worked toward them because I wanted a different destination from the one I had seen for myself on that day in September. And I learned that just because he wanted something very different from what I wanted didn't mean that I had to give up and buckle under. I made an effort to keep my dreams right where I could see them for nine months, in spite of the fact that he got meaner and more violent throughout those nine months.

Once you know the Truth, you can never (really) go back to the lie. And the Truth was—and is—that I deserve my Dreams. And I have never wanted to go back to the lie that said that I had no choice but to be a victim.

So now we come to the second foundational principle that I consciously practiced during that time. That was the idea that peace begins with me.

One of the times that I had left Jeff, I had agreed to come back only if he would go to counseling with me… (I know, I know. But this time it was different… No really, it was! This time I not only made him promise, but I made him stick to that promise—and I didn't move back in until we had seen the counselor three times and he had promised we could continue seeing her. Okay, so he refused to see her anymore after I came home. I should have known—but I was still hanging onto my dream.)

I found this counselor at Mary's church, The Living Enrichment Center (LEC), and she was wonderful! She saw through all of Jeff's little ploys and attempts to manipulate and place the blame for all of our problems on me, and she called me on some of my stuff that I'd have preferred not to admit to, also. She helped me to recognize when I was being defensive just out of habit, and, more importantly, she helped me to see when I was just rolling over and accepting the blame for things just to keep him from being mad at me or in an attempt to get his approval. She was a gifted counselor, in my opinion, and I am still grateful for all that I learned from her. One of the things that she gave me was a card (which I still have) that says, "Peace begins with me." I carried that card around in my wallet for a long time, and I pulled it out regularly to remind myself of what it said.

Try thinking about that statement as you could apply it to your own life. Peace begins with you. No matter what your spouse, sibling, parent, child, boss, coworker, or fellow motorist on the freeway is doing—peace can begin with you...or not. You can choose peace instead of this...or not. It's an amazing idea if you can grasp it and make it a habit.

Peace begins with me. I can choose peace instead of this. And it's true. I tested this principle out a lot during the last few months of my relationship with Jeff. I practiced and I practiced and I practiced. And the more I practiced, the more opportunities he gave me to practice. The more I practiced this one thing, the stronger I became. My thoughts went something along these lines:

> "Peace begins with me. I don't have to react to his button pushing. I can choose peace instead of this. I don't have to allow him to drag me into an argument. Peace begins with me. I can choose peace instead of this. I don't have to let my feelings be hurt when he tells me I'm ugly or calls me a whore. My own peace begins with **ME**. I can choose peace **inside myself** instead of this. Like Mary says in her book, "I don't have to let the petty acts of an unhappy individual damage me." I don't have to. I can if I choose to, but I don't have to. Peace begins with me. I can choose peace instead of this."

"Peace begins with me. I can choose peace instead of this." It was like a mantra that I just kept repeating over and over to myself until it became a reality for me. It was amazing. The more I decided I could choose peace, the easier it was for me not to take his mean-spiritedness personally. The more I deliberately chose peace, the more peaceful I became. The more I let go of the need to defend myself, knowing that peace really could begin with me, the less defensive I was — and the more powerful I became. Try it sometime. If you want to feel powerful, try being at peace first and you will find that the power comes of its own accord — you won't have to put any effort into it at all.

I held onto my dream of a happy and healthy relationship with that man for as long as I could. I had seen the good that was in him during the first year we were together, so I knew it was there. I didn't want to give up, and so for nine months I continued to hold onto my dream of a happy relationship with him. But as those months progressed, he proved to me more and more often that he just was not interested in figuring out how to make our relationship a healthy one. The idea of peace did not seem to appeal to him at all. As those months progressed the differences between what he wanted and what I wanted became more and more pronounced (and painful).

And then, too, there was my newfound relationship with Spirit, which was deepening nicely. I was learning to have some faith in a Higher Power that loved me. I went to LEC several times to hear Mary speak—and I learned stuff. I read and reread her book and each time I read it I learned something new about the kind of relationship I could have with God if I chose to.

Mary is a New Thought minister. (Please do not confuse New Thought with New Age—they are different.) I had never heard of New Thought, but I guess it's been around for about one-and-a-half centuries. "New Thought" is an umbrella term that covers religions such as Unity, Divine Science, and Religious Science (Science of Mind). This is how I understand New Thought: The New Thought religions (especially Science of Mind, which I know better than any of the others) are made up of all the most loving, positive, and growth producing aspects of all of the traditional religions, including but not limited to Christianity, Buddhism, Hinduism, Muslim, and Judaism.

I am now a member of a Church of Religious Science (not Scientology, although I have taken some of their courses, which I found very powerful and eye-opening), and what I believe is that there is only one God, but there are many paths to God. So if the spiritual path you choose is Christianity, Muslim, Druidism, or street hockey, then that's what works for you and that's wonderful for you. Spirituality is a personal thing and I think that when you find something that works for you, something that helps you to grow into the person you would like to be, then it is in your highest and best interest to stick with it and become the person you want to be, whether or not other people agree or approve. For myself, I am just happy that I stumbled across New Thought and a God that I can believe in and embrace with complete faith.

THAT was how powerful *Building Your Field of Dreams* was for me. I had spent my whole life bouncing back and forth between not believing in God at all and the belief that God hated me. And then at the age of thirty-four I fell into a book that was written by a real person who has had real problems and challenges and who wasn't afraid to use her own life as an example of how to view the universe as friendly even in the midst of those problems and challenges.

One of the things that Mary talked about when I first began listening to her speak at LEC — that I have never forgotten and that I regularly *use* — was Jesus talking about building your house on a solid foundation. He said that if you build your house (your Faith) on sand, when the winds and waves come your house will be washed away and you'll be left without a place to live. But if you build your house on a foundation of rock, then the winds and waves can come as they will and your house (your Faith) will remain where you placed it. Okay, that stuff is all well and good, but THIS is what she said that caught my attention and stuck in my mind, "He said *when* the winds and waves come. He did not say the winds and waves *wouldn't* come." We will all have winds and waves from time to time — there is no question of that. But how we handle those winds and waves is entirely up to us. We can build our house on sand and handle things from a place of Fear and watch everything we've built for our selves get washed away when the storm comes, or we can dig down to bedrock and live from a place of Faith.

New Thought is all about learning to look at things in a new and different way. ("A New Thought creates a New Thing." "Change your thinking, change your Life." "Peace can begin with me if that's what I choose." "I don't *have* to continue to be a victim." "I do *not* have to die at the hands of a man who claims to love me." "When you change the way you look at the world, the world you're looking at changes.")

On September 19, 1999 I discovered Mary Manin Morrissey, got a taste of her teachings, and really heard her when she said, "Don't let the *word* [God] get in your way of understanding." And for the next five weeks I practiced some of the things I had learned during that 90 minute program.

In the latter part of October 1999 I received *Building Your Field of Dreams,* and in it I discovered a God that I could believe in and partner with to create a better life for myself. I don't know how many times I read that book over the next couple of months, but it went with me everywhere. I was never without it. In fact, I carried that book with me everywhere for the next year and a half — it represented the rock on which I was building my foundation of faith.

In January of 2000 I went to LEC for the first time and I feel very fortunate that it's the practice of most — if not all — New Thought churches to go over "What We Believe" at the beginning of every year. That was the perfect time for me to be there.

I went several times between January and Easter of 2000. I will never forget that Easter service and Mary talking about the Resurrection from a New Thought perspective. I could "die" to the life I was experiencing any time I chose to. And then I could be resurrected into a whole new life. She did not say those exact words, but that was the message I received that day.

That was when the last of my depression lifted and I knew that everything would work out however it was going to work out. I think it was then that I decided to surrender and just let things be what they were. I continued to choose peace, but I let go of the anxiety that I felt about *having* to choose peace in the first place. Does that make sense? It does to me. It was a whole new and much deeper level of Peace.

Back to the dream…

My dream included another person. And that person worked actively to keep my dream from becoming a reality. (He knew what my dream was, but would never admit that there were any problems in our relationship. And if there *were* problems, then it was obvious that they were *my* problems, not his. He would say things to me like, "Yes, I slammed you against the wall and then threw you to the floor, but you should have just given me your keys. You shouldn't have tried to leave." And to his way of thinking, he was making a valid point — if I would just do what he wanted everything would be perfect.)

I was still practicing choosing peace. "Peace begins with me" is true even in that kind of situation. I wanted peace, and at that point the only way I was going to get it was to leave for good. I didn't want to live in a toxic atmosphere any more. Peace begins with me and my choices. Just because Jeff didn't want peace didn't mean that I couldn't have it for myself if I chose it!

Chapter 9 in Mary's book is called "Failure: Finding Meaning in the Defeated Dream." By June of 2000 I knew that it was sheer folly to hang on any longer. If I didn't admit to myself that I wasn't going to reach this particular dream, then I was going to die making the effort. And did I want to die for the love that I wanted from this man? Did I want to die at the hands of the man I loved? These are very tough questions to ask yourself when you're in this kind of situation.

On about June 22, 2000 I admitted defeat. I had given it an honest effort and things had gotten progressively worse. I think it was that day—June 22—that a coworker asked me if I would leave for good if I had enough money to make it work. She offered to give me $100 to help me get on my feet somewhere away from Portland. I thought about it for awhile and decided that with all I had learned about dream-building and looking at life in a new and different way, I would probably be able to leave and not go back to him if I did get out of town. My other choice was to pass on her offer and stay with him until he killed me, which would be sooner rather than later. I accepted her offer of financial help. She then proceeded to ask some of the other people that we worked with to chip in and, to my amazement, a couple of them did.

Something that should be noted: I did not give up on my dream of a happy and healthy relationship. I let go of my dream of a happy, healthy relationship with that particular man.

So I made plans over that weekend. All together I had $160 to use for my escape. On June 23rd and 24th

I snuck some essential personal things out of the travel trailer that Jeff and I were living in, and I took them to work and left them there. It was so hard to behave normally during those four days, knowing that I was planning on leaving *again,* and knowing what he would do to me if he found out.

I used the internet to figure out where I was going to go, and then I covered my tracks by deleting anything that might show any kind of history of what I had looked at. And then I made sure and checked out a bunch of places that I had no intention of going to, and I left all of that right where he could find it.

I had originally planned on going to Laughlin, Nevada because I figured it would be really easy to find a job right away. I have to say, though, that I am *extremely* grateful that I changed my mind at the last minute! I have been to Laughlin a few times — it's a great place to visit for a couple of days, but I don't know that I would want to live there.

At the last minute I decided that I would go to Mesa, Arizona. The reason? A very special and wonderful friend of mine had lived in Mesa for a while and she had been happy there. She had never really been happy in Portland, but for the six or so years that she lived in Mesa, she had actually liked her life. This gave me hope that it was possible for me to create a life for myself that I would actually like living. And since I was making it a point to go someplace where I didn't know anybody because Jeff would never believe that I would have the guts to do that, Mesa seemed as good a place as any. The other reason was that it was a place that half my money would get me to. Eighty dollars was more than I really wanted to spend, but anything less than that would not have gotten me far enough away. Anything closer would have made it too easy for him to find me. (I know, call me paranoid—but he had always found me one way or another before, and I didn't want to take any chances this time.)

So, without giving up (which is what I would have done pre-Mary Morrissey) I found it necessary to rethink my dream. I knew that I wanted a happy, healthy relationship and as I was making preparations to run for my life, a light bulb came on. That thought was this: "Maybe I should focus on being happy and emotionally healthy myself, before I go and jump into another relationship just because I can't stand being alone." Wow! What a concept! I had never tried that before. Always before when a relationship ended, I would immediately start looking for a new one. I had never been a person who enjoyed my own company. I had always hated myself and my life, and so I couldn't stand being by myself. I had always believed that I needed to be in a relationship to feel complete. It had never occurred to me before that most of the relationships I had been in had left me feeling just the opposite.

So I decided on a new Dream. And that Dream was this: "I do not want to just start over. I want to create a whole new life for myself. I want to create a life that I can love."

June 26th of the year 2000 was the day that I left my last abuser for the tenth and final time. I climbed on a Greyhound bus and I ran for my life. I ran for—and to—a whole new and completely different kind of life from the one that I had lived before!

Chapter 5

Good-bye, Old Life

"Take the first step in faith. You don't have to see the whole staircase – just take the first step."
~ Martin Luther King, Jr.

I spent Sunday, June 25, 2000 just trying to behave normally. And while I was trying to behave normally I discovered that it's easy to behave normally when everything is "normal," but as soon as you feel like you *have* to behave normally you begin to wonder, "Is this how I normally behave?" It sounds funny now, but when your life depends on you being a convincing actor, it is more frightening than anything else. I really have no idea if Jeff had a feeling that something was up or not. I was just concentrating on not doing anything that would give me away. That Sunday was a really tough day — mainly because he was nice to me all day long. That is why I wonder if he thought that maybe something was about to change. I don't know. I do know that it would have been much easier for me to get on the bus the following day if we had spent that last day the same way that previous few months had gone. But as it happened, that Sunday was pleasant. The weather was nice and we spent time outside by the duck pond. I spent the day trying to reconcile myself to leaving for good, going someplace where I didn't know anybody, and saying good-bye in my heart—both to this man that I loved and to the city that I loved. It was a *very* tough day…

Fear kept me awake that night—fear that he would wake me up in the middle of the night. If you, the person reading this, have ever been with an abusive person then you know what I mean. That is something that an abuser will do—they will wait until you're sound asleep, and then they'll wake you up and pick a fight. I didn't want to be caught off guard, so I made myself stay awake.

It wasn't as if I would have been able to sleep anyway—not with all the stuff that was running around frantically in my mind.

I spent Sunday night going over my plans for the following day. Well, that was my intention, anyway. I really spent that night in a state of panic, alternating between thoughts of, *"Oh, my God, just what do I think I'm doing?!"* and, *"Oh, my God, I can't wait to see what happens!"* Back and forth all night long… That was probably the longest night of my life. Back and forth, back and forth. *"What's going to happen to me if I do this?" "What's going to happen to me if I don't do this?"* Back and forth, all night long, not allowing myself to toss and turn because then he would know that something was wrong. It was a long, long night. *"What do I have to look forward to if I get on that bus tomorrow?" "What do I have to look forward to if I don't get on that bus tomorrow?" "Do I want to change my life? Or do I want to stay here and settle for what's familiar and within my comfort zone, even though it's painful?" "Am I doing the right thing? Or am I asking for trouble that I might not be able to deal with?"* On and on and on, back and forth… All. Night. Long.

The alarm went off at 5:00 a.m. and I dragged myself out of bed in a state of completely mixed up feelings, the strongest of which was just plain gratitude that the night was finally over. If only he hadn't been so nice the day before and reminded me of all the things that I loved about him. But I knew that he had done that before, many times, and it had always gone back to the same old thing: power and control, suspicion and accusations, anger and pain, attack and defend. Whether he had been nice the day before or not, I knew I wasn't willing to stay and be abused by him any longer. Two and a half years of that was enough for me. Comfort zone and settling be damned — I was going for it!

After he left for work, I waited. Sometimes he would turn around and come back to see what I was doing (to see if I had another man in the trailer with me) right after he left in the morning, so I knew better than to do anything other than what I normally did. So I did what I normally did at that time of the morning — I watched *Little House on the Prairie* on TV. This particular morning he didn't turn around and come back, he just called me on the phone to see what I was doing. I was thankful that I didn't have to lie…

When *Little House* was over I got busy. With my heart in my throat and my hair standing on end because I was in a state of extreme hyper-awareness (in other words, terror), just as I had been the previous September when I had found myself picking up the phone to order Mary's book, I packed a backpack and a duffel bag, which was all I would take with me to Phoenix. I had no idea what it was going to be like there, and if I did end up living on the street I didn't want to have too much to keep track of. So I tried to travel as light as possible and still have the things I would really need.

As I got dressed I made sure I had what I considered the most important things of all at that time (besides *Building Your Field of Dreams*). I made sure I had my quotes. Some people might think that was silly of me. "Quotes? What do you need quotes for? What good are quotes going to do you in a situation like this?"

And I would say *this* in response to *that*, "What good are they going to do me? They are going to help me stay focused on what I want for myself and what I need to do to get to the place I'd like to be." Days before this, I had printed out several quotes that I had been carrying around in my back pocket. Three of them, in particular, were what kept me mentally and emotionally in a place in which I was actually able to do the things I was doing that morning and not give in to the fear that was so very powerful and that would have completely overwhelmed me if I hadn't had something positive to focus on.

All three of these quotes were, and still are, equally important to me. If not for these quotes I have no doubt that I would not be alive and living the wonderful life that I am experiencing today. I used all three of them in tandem to hang on to my faith and be able to make life-giving choices for myself during what can only be considered a very rough time in my life.

The first one is a quote from Albert Einstein. He said this:

> "The significant problems we face cannot be solved at the level of thinking that created them."

The second came from William Shakespeare, who said:

> "Our doubts are traitors, and make us lose the good we
> oft might win — by fearing to attempt."

And the third, and most powerful for me, was something that Martin Luther King, Jr. said, which was:

> "Take the first step in faith. You don't have to see the
> whole staircase — just take the first step."

I had these three, and several others, printed out and tucked into my back pocket. There is no question that without them I would not have been able to take the steps that I took that morning. Thank God for those three men. They are all a part of history, but they are all alive and well in the present, too, as people like me are still listening to — and using — what they had to say.

So how did I use them? It was nothing short of miraculous how I was able to get these principles to work for me. This is so cool...

> "The significant problems we face cannot be solved at the
> level of thinking that created them."

I could see that I had several pretty significant problems. Here are just a few of them:

- I was running away from a very abusive person who also happened to be very intelligent. All it would take would be for one thing to go wrong and I would be caught and hurt — again.
- I was running away from everything I knew and loved, and I was going to a place that I had never been before and knew absolutely nothing

about except that it was going to be hot, ugly (in my opinion), and a lot bigger than what I was used to.
- After I bought my bus ticket I would only have $80 left to get started with in Arizona.
- I had not slept since the previous Saturday night and I was exhausted.
- My co-worker who was giving me the money to get away was going to be there to pick me up at 10:00 that morning. What if Jeff picked that time to show up and check on what I was doing? This was entirely possible. He had done it before, and it would be so ugly if that were to happen…

If you focus on your problems, all you see are your problems. And what you focus on, you attract more of into your life. I know this for a fact!

So, "The significant problems we face cannot be solved at the level of thinking that created those problems." I could see what my problems were, and they all seemed pretty significant to me. I had a choice to make… do I stay at the problem level, or do I move my thinking up to the solution level? I have found that if you lift your level of thinking to the solution level, a solution will usually present itself to you right away, just because you're willing to see a solution in the first place! I was in the process of taking care of my biggest problem (domestic violence) just by doing the things I was doing that morning. I knew that, and it helped me feel better in an overall kind of way. But there were still those individual things that I had to deal with, too.

The first thing I needed to do was stop worrying about things over which I had no control. If he showed up, then that would be something that would have to be handled at the time. It made absolutely no sense for me to worry that it *might* happen. I saw that right away and, although it wasn't easy and the worry did crop back up from time to time (often) that morning, I was able to let go of it every time I caught myself doing it. So I went from actually creating a problem where only a *potential* problem existed, to feeling lighter every time those thoughts came back and I was able to set them down and not carry them around with me. That problem was solved just by looking to the solution level and noticing that I was the one creating that particular problem!

As for the rest of my problems... the other two quotes took care of them.

"Our doubts are traitors, and make us lose the good we oft might win — by fearing to attempt."

I asked myself these questions whenever the Fear showed up. "What will happen for me if I don't try? *Nothing good, that's for sure!* If I listen to my Doubts and hand my power over to them, then what will happen? *I will stay stuck right where I'm at.* What is the good that I will lose if I continue to be too scared to move? *I have no idea, but I do know this... If I do not try, then I will always know that about myself. If I don't at least give it a try, then I will know that I have made a conscious choice to stay in a relationship in which I get hurt on a regular basis.*" So when my Fears showed up and tried to take control, this is what I did — and it is something that I still do to this day whenever I'm afraid of something — when my Fears showed up I looked right at them and I consciously and deliberately saw them for what they were. I said to them, "I see you. I know you're there and I know what you want. You have no power over me." I had seen Mary demonstrate this on television the previous September and I found that when I used it on purpose, it worked.

I often hear people say that they did something that scared them in spite of their fears. To me that implies a struggle, which I've had enough of in my life. I prefer to say that I did things that I was afraid of *accompanied by* fear. I am a human being, and human beings often feel fear. It does no good to fight it because when we fight our Fear, all we're doing is feeding it and making it bigger and stronger. If we can get ourselves to just accept it for what it is (False Evidence Appearing Real) and allow it to be there without giving a lot of attention to it, how much easier it is to do the thing that we're afraid of! When you stop struggling against your Fear you take the wind out of its sails. If you resist your Fear, pay attention to your Fear, feed your Fear, deny your Fear (which is basically the same as resisting it) all you're doing is giving it more and more power. But if you can bring yourself to just look at it, acknowledge it, and know that it's there, without giving a bunch of energy to it, you can move forward without a huge struggle.

I was terrified that whole morning before my coworker and her boyfriend arrived, but I was able to deal with it without becoming a basket case because I saw my fear for what it was ("monster-mind," imagination, things that *could* happen, things that *might* happen) and I didn't let it have control. It was a very empowering experience that basically set the tone for everything that followed because it let me know that I had it in me to do something that huge without breaking down and giving in to worrying about things that I couldn't control or things that may or may not happen.

> "Our doubts are traitors, and make us lose the good we
> oft might win – by fearing to attempt."

Our doubts, fears, and worries only have power in our lives if we give it to them. That Monday morning experience was the beginning, for me, of really learning that for myself. And beginning to learn that lesson for myself that day was my first little baby step on the road to my Dreams.

And this brings me to what Dr. King said:

*"Take the first step in faith. You don't have to see the whole staircase — **just take the first step**."*

How do you keep from feeding your Fear? By feeding your Faith! It is absolutely impossible to feed them both at the same time. You can know that your fear is there and deliberately take your attention off of that fear and place it on your Faith. That is how you get past the barriers of worry, doubt, fear, and thoughts of, "Oh, my God, I don't think I'm strong enough to do this!" It has to be a deliberate thing. You look at your Fear and see it for whatever mechanism it happens to be for you (self-preservation, self-protection, comfort-zone, just plain laziness, etc.). You say to it, "I see you. I know who you are and I know what you want. You have no power over me. If I listen to you I will never have the life that I really want to be living. If I listen to you, I will never realize my dreams — they will just continue to be something I dream about." And then you look to your Faith. And then you take *that* step. You really *don't* have to see the whole staircase.

As you take that first step of Faith you begin to know for yourself that you *can* take that step, and so you can bring yourself to take the *next* step, and before you know it you're on that Greyhound bus on your way to a whole new life. Or you're on that Harley riding around the state of Arizona. Or you're jumping out of that airplane. Or you're selling your first painting. Or you're opening your very own tattoo parlor. Or you're investing in your first house that you want to fix up and sell. It doesn't matter what your dream is. You will never realize it if you cannot bring yourself to see your fear, acknowledge it for what it is, and then take whatever steps you need to take in Faith.

That Monday morning in Portland I could not have known what my life would be like today. All I knew that morning was that I dreamed of living a life in which I didn't have to be afraid of a person who claimed to love me. I knew that I dreamed of a life of happiness instead of pain. I knew that I dreamed of a life in which I was able to talk to my children whenever I wanted to and not feel like I was doing something wrong. I knew that I dreamed of a life in which I felt good about myself. These were things that I knew I wanted in my life, and that step up into that bus was my first step in Faith.

As I took that step I deliberately placed my focus on Dr. King's words. I am not just speaking figuratively here. I mean that as I *physically* stepped up into the bus I was reciting to myself, "Take the first step in Faith. You don't have to see the whole staircase — just take the first step. You don't have to see the whole staircase. You don't have to see the whole staircase — just take the first step. Have faith in yourself. You are stepping into a whole new life, even if you don't know right now what that life will look like. You don't have to see the whole staircase. By taking this step, you are stepping into something new and wonderful just because you are able to take this one step right here." That was a very positive experience for me because — probably for the first time in my life, really — I had set aside the negative, fear-based stuff that I *could* have focused on, and instead put my attention on the positive things that I *wanted* to happen for me — even if I was only able to see it in a hazy, vague, unclear sort of way. I really didn't need to see the whole staircase. I could find positive things to focus on right here, right now, and the rest of the staircase would take care of itself as I moved along in my life.

And something I have learned over the last several years is this: I will never see the whole staircase! Why? Because *I am creating my own staircase* step by step, choice by choice, Dream by Dream as I go along with my life! Just as my road is my road and I am in control of my own steering wheel whether I want to admit that to myself or not, my staircase is my staircase and it will lead wherever my own steps take me. So, just as my road has twists and turns, my staircase has ups and downs because I — as a human being — am not perfect and this Faith stuff does take practice.

I heard a lady named Dr. Peggy Conger give a wonderful and extremely simple definition of the word "fear" once, and it is so appropriate to what I'm talking about here. She said this:

"Fear is Faith in the negative."

This is SO true! And there are two different ways that you can look at it. One of them is this: Fear is a negative use of Faith. And the other is: Fear is faith that something negative is going to happen.

Taking this into account you can see why our staircases will have ups and downs. I am not perfect and I don't claim to have always taken my steps "in Faith," but that Greyhound bus experience taught me that I *could* let go and just Trust, and since then I have spent less and less time and energy on the "downs" in my staircase. It's actually quite fascinating to look back over the last several years and see exactly where I took the Fear steps and exactly where I took the Faith steps.

So I have learned that:

"Our doubts are traitors, and make us lose the good we oft might win — by fearing to attempt."

Goes hand in hand with:

"Take the first step in faith. You don't have to see the whole staircase — just take the first step."

Each of those quotes compliments the other, and that is how I used them. And that is how I continue to use them to this day.

It starts with the "significant problem," which leads to the Fear, which takes me to the creation of another step in my staircase. Whether it's a step "down" into Fear, or a step "up" in Faith is completely up to me.

That Monday, June 26th of the year 2000 I took a step "up" into a place of Faith. I made a choice that morning to see what I was doing as an adventure and to take whatever happened along the way as a lesson and to learn whatever I could from it. I made a choice to trust my Faith, to focus on my Faith, and to surrender to my Faith. I also (constantly) reaffirmed my choice to believe that I live in a friendly universe — that I live in a universe that wants me to win, that wants me to be happy and live my Dreams.

That bus ride was a *profound* experience for me. Talk about lessons learned! I consider it one great big thirty-seven hour learning experience. But it is something I never would have experienced if I hadn't been able to get myself to step up into that bus in the first place.

Pop Your Paradigm!

Chapter 6

The (Bus) Ride of My Life!

"Gratitude is one of the sweet shortcuts to finding peace of mind and happiness inside. No matter what's going on outside of us, there's always something we could be grateful for."
~ Barry Neil Kaufman

My coworker and her boyfriend picked me up that morning and took me to the bus station, where I lived my life for the next hour with my Fear (terror) *looming* over me like a monstrous shadow blocking any light that tried to reach me. It wasn't just whispering in my ear, it was screaming frantically in my face.

"What do you think you're doing?! Don't you understand what's going to happen to you if he figures out what you're doing?! There are so many, many doors in this place – there's no way you can watch them all!! What if you don't see him come in and he comes up behind you?! They made you give your real name when you bought your ticket, and they couldn't guarantee that they wouldn't give out your information if he asked. He's not stupid, you know. What if he comes in here after you leave and finds out where you're going

and is waiting for you when you get off the bus in Phoenix?! Huh? Then what will you do?! Why don't you save yourself the trouble and just go back to the trailer park and pretend you never even considered this? You are such a fool if you think you're going to get away with this pitiful attempt to improve your life. You know it's not going to work! You know something's going to happen to ruin it. You know it's not possible for you to ever be happy or successful at anything, so why are you doing this to yourself?"

On and on and on, for the eternity (the hour) that I had to stay in the lobby of the bus station waiting to get onto my bus—that voice did not shut up once.

And it didn't help at all that my cellular phone kept ringing. It was him checking on me to see what I was doing. I am still amazed that I was able to go against my conditioning and not answer whenever he called. Especially with the Fear there screaming at me that every time I didn't answer, I was making my punishment that much worse. How did I know that he wasn't calling me from just outside the bus station? How did I know that he wasn't watching me from somewhere where I couldn't see him? How did I know that he wasn't watching to catch me deliberately not answering, so he could use that against me? I thought about just shutting off my phone, but I couldn't get myself to do it. I needed to know what he was up to. Every time he called he left a message, each more angry than the last. I checked every one of them as soon as he left them. That way I had some sort of an idea whether or not he knew where I was. The angrier he became, the more certain I was that he hadn't figured it out yet. I knew that if he left me a calm message—that would be the end of me, because that would mean that he was watching from somewhere near me. It seems a little weird, but as long as he was leaving angry, you'd-better-answer-your-phone-or-else, messages, I knew that I was somewhat okay. It was the most effective way I had to monitor what he was doing.

It's amazing — just sitting here *writing* about this I can feel my eyeballs bulging in their sockets as I'm remembering that experience. I can remember that feeling — as if my eyeballs were going to pop out of their sockets — as I tried so very hard to watch every door into the bus station.

I kept repeating to myself — over and over and over again:

> *"Our doubts are traitors, and make us lose the good we oft might win – by Fearing to attempt. What will my life be like if I don't at least try to make this work? I see you, Fear. I know who you are and I know what you want. The only power you have over me is the power that I hand to you. You just want me to take the easy way out. Yes, it would be easier to go back to my little box of a life and stay in it and feel sorry for myself because my life is so awful! It would be easy to stay stuck and give up, but I'm not willing to live that life anymore and it's worth it to me to go to this trouble – to expend this energy – to get myself unstuck and into an easier (hopefully) life."*

Have you ever seen a vehicle that's stuck in the mud? And then watched it get itself *unstuck* from that mud? It has to expend a tremendous amount of energy, and for a time the wheels just spin as the engine revs. But when the tires finally catch hold of something to grab onto, the vehicle then *explodes* out of the mud, and there's no stopping it.

That was what waiting to get on the bus felt like to me. I was in the process of breaking away from what was keeping me stuck, and in that process I was forced to sustain a very high level of energy for an indefinite period of time. My Fear was huge and very, very real. And it was there the entire time—it did not let up even once. As I waited there in my sustained terror, I could feel my blood pressure going up higher and higher. I'm kind of amazed that I didn't have a stroke right there in that lobby!

Finally, after that eternity that was really only an hour, it was 11:15 and time to board the bus. *(Take the first step in Faith...) Then* it became a little easier to breathe. At least I wouldn't be out in the open anymore, and the bus windows were tinted, so if he did show up it would take some effort for him to find me. And soon we would be pulling out of the station and I would no longer have to worry about being dragged off the bus by my hair (that was where my imagination repeatedly took me). As I sat down in my seat I was finally able to take a real breath. In a few minutes we would be leaving, and *then* I would be able to relax somewhat.

I called my daughter, Melissa, who was seventeen at the time, and told her what I was doing and that I was on my way out of Portland. I told her I was shutting off my phone and that I wasn't going to turn it back on until I got to Phoenix. She was worried about me, but glad to see me taking some action to get away. She was also very, very skeptical about whether or not I would be successful. After all, I had left this man *nine times* before this, and gone back to him every single time. At this point both of my kids had said to me, "Yeah, right Mom. You talk about leaving him for good all the time. I'll believe it when I see it." So she was hopeful that I would be successful, while at the same time not really believing that I *could* be successful. But she was as supportive as she was able to be, keeping her fingers crossed for me. I was grateful that she understood why I felt that I needed to get away from Portland. She and I both knew that if I stayed in town I would forever resemble a ping-pong ball, bouncing back and forth and back and forth, in and out of that relationship, never able to find any emotional health or balance.

After everyone had boarded, the driver started the engine, and I took an even deeper breath. I was on my way! For better or for worse, no matter what happened, I was on my way to a whole new life! Or so I thought.

As I sat there waiting in anticipation for the bus to back out of the terminal, I could feel the excitement and fear warring with each other for the domination of my thoughts. *I'm so scared! I'm so excited! I'm so scared! I'm so excited! What's going to happen to me?! I don't know, but it's definitely going to be interesting! How I handle whatever does happen to me will be completely up to me!*

Waiting, waiting, waiting for that bus to pull out of the station... But it just sat there. I thought maybe the driver was just warming up the engine for a few minutes. *I'm so scared! I'm so excited! I'm so scared! I'm so excited!* A few minutes turned into about fifteen minutes. The "scared" was getting the better of the "excited"...

After fifteen minutes of sitting there with the engine running, try to imagine what my feelings were as I watched the driver shut off the ignition, get out of his seat, and leave! Without saying a word to us passengers to let us know what was going on, he got off the bus and walked away. And he didn't come back! We sat there on that bus for *an hour and a half!* No one ever came to tell us what was going on. I have no idea why no one got off the bus to go find out. I don't think anybody actually expected that we would be sitting there that long.

I knew there was no way in hell I was getting out of my seat and risking that bus pulling out without me. I can tell you—emphatically!—that sitting there for that ninety minutes *WAS* hell. So I mean it quite literally when I say, "There was no way in hell..." I was in hell. That was all there was to it. I had expended so much energy that morning to actually get myself onto that bus without having a nervous breakdown. And then I had experienced feelings of such excitement and anticipation when the engine started, followed by bewilderment and confusion when the engine shut off, and then more confusion and bewilderment as I watched the driver walk away from the bus and into the building. Saying I felt let down would be a just a *little* bit of an understatement. It would be more accurate to say that I felt like somebody had pulled the rug out from under me, or that the wind had been knocked out of me. It wasn't so bad at first. I thought maybe his bowels all of a sudden gave him a problem and he needed to go to the bathroom. That was the most logical thing that came to my mind. Never in a million years would I have thought that I'd be sitting there for an hour and a half waiting for him to come back. As those ninety minutes went by I made a sincere effort to control my thoughts and not lose my mind.

> *How I handle whatever happens to me will be completely up to me!*

I felt as if I were being tested. I had gotten myself this far, but now I had been stopped in my tracks. It felt as if my life was laughing at me.

*Ha! You thought you were actually going to accomplish this. You idiot! Jackass! Stupid, stupid woman! You know the longer this bus sits here, the more likely it is that he'll go home and see that you've left and figure out where you are. You know that, don't you? Foolish woman! You knew you were stupid to even consider that you might be able to make a better life for yourself. What ever made you decide to even try it? Oh yeah! You heard a **minister** say that we all deserve to have our dreams come true. Stupid woman! You forgot that you were not included in that "all," didn't you? You forgot that you were never meant to be happy or in control of your own life, didn't you? Fool! Now what are you going to do? Any second he's going to climb onto this bus and get in your face! You know that, don't you? And when that happens there will be nowhere for you to run. You are trapped right here. And when he shows up you know what's going to happen, don't you? Sure you do. He's going to be charming. He's going to be pitiful. He's going to say, "I love you, I need you, please don't leave me." And nobody on this bus will know the truth of the matter, which will be what will happen to you when he gets you away from all these people. And if you **don't** get off with him when he shows up, you know where he'll be later, don't you? Bingo! He'll be at the Greyhound station in Phoenix when you climb down those steps tomorrow night. He'll be waiting for you and then you'll be dead. You know that don't you? Well, don't you? You are so stupid to have tried this. Why don't you just give up now? You know this is a sign that it's not meant for you to be successful in this attempt to improve your life. This bus is not going to start until you give up and go home. You are not meant to have a good life. You are meant to* *be in pain until the day you die, and then you are going to die at the hands of the man that you love. That is the way of things and you know it! Why don't you just accept it and give up on this pitiful attempt at making a better life for yourself?*

If it hadn't been for Mary Morrissey and *Building Your Field of Dreams* and all of the improvements to my life that I had made over the previous nine months by applying the things I had learned from that book, I probably really would have taken those ninety minutes as a sign that it wasn't meant for me to leave Portland. Then again, without Mary and her book I never would have found the strength to get on that bus in the first place. And THAT was what I held onto during that dark place of fear and anxiety and not understanding what was going on. I kept hearing Mary say, "He (Jesus) never said there wouldn't be winds and waves. But if you build your house on a solid foundation, the winds and waves can come as they may, and your house will remain standing." I hung onto that. I needed to have faith, and I needed to trust my faith, and I needed to remember that how I handled this situation was my choice. I cannot honestly say that I was able to relax during that time of waiting and wondering what was going on. My Fear was entirely too huge for that. But neither did I give in to that Fear even though it hammered at me for an hour and a half.

During those ninety minutes I practiced remembering to breathe, while trying not to hyperventilate at the same time (picture *that!*). I thought the young lady sitting next to me probably thought I was insane. But then again, I knew that she had heard my conversation with Melissa, so I figured she might have at least *some* idea of what was going on with me during that time.

To this day I am thankful that I had no idea that the bus I was making my escape on would sit there for that amount of time without anybody letting us know what was going on. I probably would have run screaming into a nervous breakdown if I had known that I was in for that kind of sustained fear-anxiety-hopefulness-anger-pain-confusion-bewilderment-excitement-anticipation-rage at the Greyhound people for not telling us what the situation was. It was intense, to say the least!

We never did find out what that was all about. Ninety minutes (another eternity) after our driver got off the bus and walked away, he climbed back onto the bus, sat down in his seat, started the engine, and backed away from the building. He offered not one word of explanation and it still seems incredible to me that no one asked him about it. He just came back like nothing ever happened and we went on our way. It was very weird! (Did that mean I had passed the test? It sure did feel like it!)

So at about 1:30 that afternoon I was finally on my way out of Portland. This was a wonderful thing because I didn't know if I could emotionally deal with anything else that might look like something that could stop me from escaping. When that bus began moving I felt like celebrating or standing up and imitating a cheerleader — something to help release the tension that had been building and building in me during the previous four or five days.

Yes, I felt like celebrating…for about 10 minutes I felt fantastic. I felt as if I could accomplish anything. I felt powerful and proud of myself. I felt anticipation for the future — I was excited to find out what was in store for me and what I would do with whatever showed up in my life. Those 10 minutes were wonderful.

And then Fear showed its face to me again. It only took that few minutes for me to fall right back into the fear, negativity, self-pity, anger, and blame that had been my way of experiencing my life for most of my life.

> *Oh, my God, what have I done now?! I am leaving everything I know and love to go to a place where I don't know anybody and I have no idea what's going to happen to me. Why does my life have to be this way? Why does it have to be so impossible for me to find happiness? How come I always have to be the one to leave? Why can't these guys take the words, "I don't want to be in a relationship with you any more." for what they really mean? I don't want to have to run away. Why couldn't he have just left me alone all those times that I left him before? If he had just left me alone, then I wouldn't be here now, watching everything that I know and love go by at 60 miles an hour, possibly never to be seen by me again. Why does my life have to be this way? Why? Why? Why? Now just look at me, watching Oregon fly by on the other side of this window. It shouldn't have to be this way. Why couldn't he have just been nice to me? Why couldn't he have treated me like he loved me? He SAID he loved me all the time, but then he would always turn around and say something hateful or humiliating with his next breath. I shouldn't have to live that way! I just want to be happy, and now look what I'm doing. I'm leaving everything that I love: my kids, what friends I have left, the beauty of my home state, a job that I like… I'm being forced to leave everything behind and go to a place that I've never been to before. I'm going there all by myself and the only thing*

> *I know about that place is that it's brown and it's hot and it's huge. Look at all that green out there on the other side of this window. It's going by so fast! I might never see green like this again. I hate my life! Why did I ever have to be born?*

I cried. I cried *hard*. From Portland to Roseburg, I cried off and on. I cried because I was scared. I cried because I was tired. I cried because I was watching my beautiful home state go by outside and I had no idea if I would ever see it again. I cried because I was getting farther and farther away from my children and I didn't know if I would ever have a chance to be close to them again. I cried because my son didn't even know that I had left, and I hadn't been able to say goodbye. I cried because I was torturing myself with thoughts of, "What if this is a huge mistake?" I cried because I knew I was hurting Jeff by doing what I was doing, and I really didn't want to hurt him, but I couldn't think of anything else I could do to prevent myself from being hurt by *him*. I cried because, even though he was abusive a lot of the time, we *had* had some good times together, and with my leaving I knew there was no chance of ever having a good time with him again. I cried. I cried because I was giving up *everything* that I knew and loved, and for what? I had no idea. I cried because I needed to cry. And when I was finished I felt hollow and empty and depressed. I felt like a victim, as I had for my entire life. I seemed to have left all of my positive, optimistic thoughts back in Portland with my kids and the green grass and trees and beauty. I was upset and deeply, deeply depressed.

Remember the dried out sponge that I talked about in Chapter 3? Well, sponges dry out if you don't keep them wet, don't they? That's what I had done to myself here. I had removed myself from what had been filling me with life and I had dried right back up again. But the thing about dried up sponges is this—you can always get them wet again! Isn't that the most wonderful thing you've ever heard?!

As I was looking out the window and crying my eyes out because I thought I might never see anything green again, the young lady sitting next to me kept saying, "I can't WAIT to get away from all this *green!*" Looking back now it's kind of funny, but at the time I was just annoyed. That little girl just plain annoyed me all the way around. She looked about seventeen, and she was excited about everything. She was happy. She smiled all the time. I looked at her and saw how young and pretty and happy she was and I thought to myself, *"You just wait. One of these days something is going to happen to you, and then you'll know that life isn't all flowers and candy and soda pop. Some day something will happen that will wipe that smile off your face permanently and for all time. And I feel sorry for you when that does happen."* I thought how sad it was that life had to be that way, and I hoped she would enjoy it while she could—I just wished she would find another seat to enjoy it in! (At this point in my journey I had completely forgotten that I had decided that I live in a friendly universe. I was fully in my "victim consciousness" and my place that said "my life hates me." When you're standing in *that* place, everything looks bad to you.)

But gradually her positive attitude began to penetrate my depressed state. It was that, "I can't wait to get away from all this *green.*" That sentence, repeated every once in a while, was what finally, really came into my awareness and got me thinking about things in a different way. There I was, upset about leaving what

I thought was the most beautiful place in the world, sitting next to a young lady who couldn't wait to get away from that very same place because she couldn't stand looking at it. Her name was Cynthia and she was from the Los Angeles area — had lived there all her life, I think — and she was literally overwhelmed by the green of the Pacific Northwest. As she kept making that statement over and over again, at first I was irritated. I was fully in my "victim consciousness" and I was comfortable there. I didn't want to cheer up, dammit, I was depressed and that was where I wanted to wallow for a while! And that's what I did — for a while... for exactly as long as I chose to.

It was the combination of *Building Your Field of Dreams* and Cynthia at the beginning of this trip that made my life today possible. I learned so much during those two days on that bus!

There I was, sitting in my window seat, wallowing in my self-pity, crying because I thought I'd never see beauty again. Meanwhile, the young woman sitting in the seat immediately to my left was looking out that very same window at the very same things, but she was seeing something completely different from what I was seeing! I saw beauty. Cynthia saw something that she couldn't wait to get away from. I was upset to be leaving. She was so happy to be leaving that she was practically bouncing up and down in her seat.

As that bus continued South on Interstate 5 and I began to see less and less green, I became more and more depressed. As that bus continued South on Interstate 5 and Cynthia began to see more and more brown, she became happier and happier.

This got me thinking. Mary talks about the lens that we look at life through, and I was just beginning to learn that how I handled things that showed up in my life was completely up to me. And one of the things that determined how I handled things was my *perception* of those things. If I looked at a situation expecting to see something bad, well, guess what I would see! If I looked out that bus window expecting to see ugliness at the end of my journey, then that would be exactly what I would find. And I *had* gotten on that bus with the expectation of leaving beauty behind and seeing things get uglier and uglier as we got closer and closer to Arizona. And that was exactly what I was experiencing! And it sucked just as much as I had expected it to!

But then there was Cynthia, looking at things from *her* seat, from her point of view and with her expectations and perceptions.

We were two different people experiencing the same exact thing, but my interpretation of what I was experiencing was the exact opposite of Cynthia's interpretation of what she was experiencing, even though — in reality — what we were both experiencing was one and the same thing… The *only* difference was in the perception of the person having the experience.

So I got to thinking, "What if I try looking at things differently? What if I stop *expecting* things to be ugly? What would happen if I started looking for beauty in whatever I see outside my window?" And then I thought of the quotes that I had stuck in my back pocket, and that I had put them there for just this kind of situation, to help me find a new perspective whenever I got stuck in this kind of mindset — to help me get my mind "unset" and find a different way of looking at things. I pulled them out of my pocket and just picked one at random, trusting that it would be something helpful. And this is what I saw:

> "Where I place my attention, I am placing my intention."
> ~ Mary Manin Morrissey

And that was the perfect thing for me to come across right then. It was amazingly appropriate and seemed to speak directly to what I was right in the middle of experiencing. I remembered hearing Mary talk about this in the *Building Your Dreams* program on Oregon Public Broadcasting. What it said to me as I came across it right then on that bus was that what you focus on, you attract more of into your experience. If I placed my attention only on the fact that I was leaving what I loved, then THAT would be my experience. But if I could turn it around and place my attention on something more positive, then my experience would be completely different. Where I chose to place my attention was entirely up to me...

I have had people say to me since then, "How can I change my life just by changing how I think about things? That won't work—it's not possible!" And I have to say to them that they are right. As long as they keep their attention on *it's not possible*, then that is what their experience will be.

I learned for myself during those two days on the bus that you really can improve your life by placing—and keeping—your attention on *improving your life*.

Okay, yes, it was easier to talk to myself about it than it was to actually do it. I discovered that right away. So I focused my attention on finding a way to get this to work for me. I decided to open my book (which I was coming to think of as my best friend) at random and see what I would see. As I did that, I found Mary talking about gratitude. She says that when you focus on what you have to be grateful for, "...you can see more than what you do not have. You can appreciate what you have and make room for all that is forthcoming." This felt like something I should pay attention to. I decided to try it and see what happened. I decided to place my attention on this thought:

> *I have far more in my life to be grateful for than I do to complain about.*

As I deliberately focused my attention on things that I could appreciate and feel grateful for, I found that more and more things showed up that I could appreciate and feel grateful for! I started out with little things like, *"I am so happy that I haven't had to go into the bathroom on this bus!"* and *"I'm very glad that the sun is shining and the sky is blue."* I had to start out with small things like that because those were things I was genuinely thankful for. If I had tried to be appreciative of "bigger" things it wouldn't have felt honest and it would have been really difficult to keep it up. By starting out with small things — things that I really did feel thankful for — and working my way up to bigger and more significant things, I was able to sustain it and keep it going and really *feel* it. It was like a magnet attracting more and more to it. By starting out small and honest I wasn't trying to force anything to be something that it wasn't. In the beginning I couldn't honestly say I was grateful to be leaving everything I knew and loved behind, but I *could* honestly say, *"I am so grateful that it's not raining on top of everything else I'm experiencing right now."* By focusing on things like that I was able to find more and more things like that to appreciate, and then I was able to really mean it when I said that I have far more in my life to be grateful for than I do to complain about.

That little girl sitting next to me had a lot to do with my figuring this out. She was so excited and happy about everything. And she was very talkative. She talked a lot about how happy she was going to be to see her kids. *(Kids? She's only about 17 and she's talking like she has several kids... I know they're starting young these days, but my goodness!)* After she had made several comments that made it sound like she had a bunch of them, I finally had to ask, "How many kids do you have?"

"Four."

"No way! How old is your oldest?"

"Nineteen..."

"Nah uh! You are only about seventeen yourself — how can you have a nineteen-year-old?!" I pretty much called her a liar.

She asked me if I'd like to see her ID, and I said I would because there wasn't any other way she was going to convince me that she was telling the truth.

She took her wallet out of her purse and then her driver's license out of her wallet. And then she handed me her license. As I looked at her birth date and did the math, my whole life changed. Actually it was my vision of what my future could be like that changed.

That "little girl" was *thirty-eight* years old... That "little girl" was three years **OLDER** than me! I was shocked and I was speechless.

That was when she started talking to me about her history. And I was in just the place and the frame of mind to be able to really hear what she was telling me.

Cynthia — this happy-go-lucky young lady who had been practically bouncing up and down in her seat with excitement — had been a victim of domestic violence. She had experienced abuse at the hands of a man who claimed to love her. She had experienced a lot of the same things that I had experienced in my life. She had also been forced to run, and she had done it with four small children! But she did it, and in doing it, she created a whole new life for herself and her kids. And she was *happy!* So my question to her was, "How are you able to be so happy? How come you're not bitter?"

And she said to me, "I'm happy because it's my choice to be happy."

She and I had an hours-long conversation about this that basically boiled down to her saying that she had figured out that how she experienced her life was completely up to her. She had discovered that she could choose how she saw things that happened in her life. In the words of Mary Morrissey, from *Building Your Field of Dreams*, Cynthia found out for herself that she could "make a stand for better over bitter." All she did was decide she wanted to look for the good things instead of focusing on the negatives. And that was where she made her stand. She decided that she wanted a better life — not a bitter life — and she stuck with that decision. And where she had placed her *attention*, was where she had placed her *intention*. Sitting right there *in the seat next to me* was living proof that the principles that I had read about over and over in *Building Your Field of Dreams* really worked! How's that for coincidence?! That young woman was *exactly* the person I needed to have in that seat next to me, even though she had never even heard of Mary Manin Morrissey. Hearing her story, and how closely her life resembled my own, and then hearing what she had done to change her life for the better was *huge* for me. Here was the proof I needed that it was possible for me to have a good life — that I could create a good life for *myself*.

In the stack of quotes in my back pocket was one from Mary Morrissey that said this:

"My history need not determine my destiny."

Right there in the seat next to me was my proof that this was true. Right there next to me was a person who had the same kind of history that I had, right down to a lot of the same experiences. But she had decided that she didn't want to continue living (surviving) the same life over and over again. She made a choice not to let her history determine what her future would be. She said something along these lines to herself, "Just because my life has been like this in the past does not mean that it has to continue to be like this. Just because this has been how I've always done it doesn't mean I have to keep doing it this way. Obviously the way I've always done it doesn't work. I need to change how I do things…"

Cynthia figured out that if she wanted to change her life, *she* had to be the one to change her life. That was the key. If she wanted to change her life it had to be up to her. No one else could do it for her, and if she stayed with her husband, expecting (hoping for) something different from him than what she was getting, she was going to die at the hands of a man who said that he loved her. If she continued to do what she had always done, she was going to continue to get what she had always gotten. She decided that what she had always gotten was not what she wanted to keep getting.

And that had been my whole reason for getting on the bus and heading for Phoenix. What I had always done had never gotten me a life of happiness. I had climbed up the steps of that bus with the intention of using all the things that I had learned during the previous months to actually do things differently. I did not want to continue getting what I had always gotten. I knew I had to try something new, and getting on the bus was my first step.

I used to believe in coincidence—I don't anymore. There's no way in hell that it was a coincidence that *that* woman sat next to me on that bus. She was the Teacher that I needed just then. And she was my proof that I was on the right track. *Everything* she said was a confirmation that the stuff that I was just beginning to learn about really worked: Everything from forgiveness and letting go, to focusing on positives, to looking for things to be grateful for instead of things that would cause her pain. And all of these things came up in our conversation *after* I had made those decisions for myself. So hearing her talk about those very things was like a confirmation for me that I had made a healthy, positive shift in my direction by making those decisions.

I think the biggest and most valuable thing that I learned directly and forcefully from Cynthia had to do with happiness. This is something that Mary talks about all the time, and it's wonderful to hear somebody talk about it and think that maybe it's possible that it could be true. But, once again, here was my living proof—here was my flesh-and-blood example. What Mary says, and what Cynthia had discovered for herself, and what I was in the process of learning was this: My happiness comes from inside me. My happiness does not depend on anything outside myself. This is what Cynthia learned for herself when she left her husband. She learned that her happiness depended only on her and it was her choice to live happy or not.

This is huge! I have learned to live my life from this place more often than not. Of course I forget sometimes, and when I do forget it always ends up being worth it because of the lessons that I learn. But still, my life is much more enjoyable when I remember where my happiness really comes from.

Think about this, if I depend on things outside myself to "make me happy" then I am handing my *ability* to be happy over to things outside myself. If I allow things outside myself to upset me, then what does that mean I'm doing with my power? I'm handing it over to *circumstances* and I am saying to those circumstances, "Please don't do anything to hurt me. Please make me happy." Well, do *circumstances* care whether I'm happy or not? Of course they don't. It's not even *possible* for circumstances to care whether I'm happy or not. Why? Because they're just circumstances. Think of the view out the bus window. That was just a circumstance. It was what it was — it was nothing more and nothing less than what Cynthia and I saw when we looked at it. But our *perception* of what we saw came from inside each of us. I saw what I saw and said, "This makes me unhappy." Cynthia saw what she saw and said, "This makes me so happy!"

But what about other people, whose actions can affect us? Okay, good question. And my answer to that is that how we deal with things is completely up to us. How we look at things is up to us.

Think about this. The things that other people do are not about me. If someone commits a crime against me, it's not about me. It's about *them*. The physical abuse that I suffered as a child had nothing to do with me except that I happened to be the child that it happened to. But that abuse was not *about* me at all — it was never about me, it was always, and only, about the person who was doing the abusing. If I hadn't been there, another child would have been abused instead of me. It wasn't about *me*, I just happened to be the one that was there. The sexual abuse that I experienced as a child was not about me, it was about the person doing the molesting. None of the domestic violence that I experienced was ever really about me, and do you know why? It's because I was not responsible for *their* feelings, actions, or choices. In all of those abusive relationships, the abuse was not about me. I just happened to be the woman in the relationship with that particular man at that particular time. If it hadn't been me, it would have been somebody else being hurt by them because it wasn't about *me* at all. Ever.

In talking with other survivors of domestic violence I have discovered that most abusers say to their victim at some point, "Why do you make me do this to you?" They say things like, "If only you wouldn't make me so angry, then I wouldn't have to hurt you." "If you would just make me happy, then I wouldn't get so angry and lose control." "If you had just willingly had sex with me, then I wouldn't have had to force you." In other words, "I am placing the responsibility for my happiness on you, and if you mess up or you don't do something that I want you to do, or if you do something that I *don't* want you to do, then you are in big trouble and I am not responsible for my actions." They justify their actions by making others responsible for their emotions. And then, of course, that makes others responsible for their actions because their actions are a result of their emotions.

Domestic violence abusers are not the only people who do this. They are just on the extreme end of that kind of thinking. Pay attention in your daily life and you will see this kind of thing everywhere. You will see parents doing it to their children. You will see children doing it to their parents. You will see it between teachers and students and between employers and employees. You will see it between customers and cashiers and between people driving on the road. It's an amazing thing to watch when you become aware of it. And it all boils down to people not taking responsibility for their own happiness.

It boils down to people making things *outside themselves* responsible for their happiness. It boils down to people handing their ability to be happy over to other people and circumstances outside of themselves.

Just as my peace begins with me, any true happiness that I want to experience can only begin with me.

Cynthia had learned that she could be happy and have a positive attitude in any situation. She did not have to depend on other people to do what she wanted them to in order for her to be happy. Even if she was in a situation that she did not like all that much, like being surrounded by all that *green,* she could still find things to be happy about because she *wanted* to be happy in the first place. And in the second place she knew that she could be happy in any circumstance or situation because she had found that she didn't have to depend on things outside herself for her happiness.

So meeting Cynthia was like a physical, flesh-and-blood reinforcement of the things I was reading about in *Building Your Field of Dreams*. Meeting her was proof that I was on the right track, and I was — and will always be — very, very grateful for that. It was an *awesome* experience that I will always remember and cherish.

All through that Monday afternoon we talked, and I learned stuff, and the sponge that was me filled back up again with healthy, juicy optimism and my sense of adventure began to return.

When the sun went down and I couldn't see anything out the window anymore, I tried to sleep. HA! That was a joke. Yes, I had learned stuff and I did feel a lot better about my choice to leave Jeff, but there was still a very real possibility that he could figure out where I went and be waiting for me when I got off the bus in Phoenix. The guy I bought my ticket from could not honestly tell me that they wouldn't give my information out if someone came in and asked. This did not seem right to me — it still doesn't — but there was nothing I could do about it except hope that it didn't happen. I tried not to stress out about it, but the fear was really big and really insistent. I did not sleep.

That whole night was a night of realizations and growth for me. Cynthia slept, so I had nothing to do but think and make decisions about what I wanted my life to look like from then on. And that's what I did.

I made three huge decisions for myself that night. I decided I would never be a victim again, which meant that I would no longer depend on other people or circumstances to make me happy. I decided I would do my best to look for positives in any and all situations and that I would be a positive person myself. And I decided that I wanted to be myself no matter what.

Now that last one was really big because I had no idea what "being myself" meant. I had spent my entire life trying to make other people happy by being what they wanted me to be, or by *not* being what they *didn't* want me to be. And when I wasn't doing that, I was spending enormous amounts of time and energy working at proving my abusers wrong when they said I was a piece of shit. (That *never* worked because they *wanted* to think that about me, so they were going to think that about me no matter what I did to try and prove them wrong. What a waste of time and energy!)

So that gave me something to think about all night long.

Who am I really? How do I want to spend my life? What kind of people do I want to spend time with?

Am I really shy, like I've always told myself, or have I always kept quiet because I've been afraid of what people would think of me if I said what I really thought?

Boy, did *that* have the ring of Truth to it! That thought came wandering through my mind in the middle of the night and it caught me off guard.

Oh, wow! Is that what I've always done? Have I ever honestly been myself? Oh, maybe here and there, but never for any length of time. I've always been so concerned with getting other people to like me (or maybe it was to keep them from disliking me?) that I've never even considered seeing if I liked myself. In fact, I've always disliked myself intensely because I didn't seem able to be what everybody else thought I should be. I have never given myself a chance! I wonder what would happen if I made that a part of this journey that I'm on right now. What would happen if I practiced being myself and not caring what other people think about me? After all, I have decided not to look outside myself for my happiness, what better place to start than right here within myself? If I'm going to create a whole new life for myself why not focus on my happiness and let whatever happens come from THAT place? Where I place my Attention I am placing my Intention. If I place my Attention on my happiness, doesn't that make happiness my Intention? Can I do that? Can I break a life-long pattern of victimhood and being a people-pleaser? Can I learn to like myself after a lifetime of NOT liking myself? I honestly don't know, but I can give it a try, can't I? If I'm going to create a whole new life for myself, I want it to be a life in which I am happy, don't I? And if I'm not happy with myself, how can I be happy with anything else? There is no way this will work for me if I can't bring myself to start here, within myself.

And what about this? What if one of the reasons I have never been happy with myself or liked myself is that I've always known deep down that I wasn't being true to myself? Wouldn't it be awesome if it was really that simple?

Okay, here is my choice: I am going to be myself no matter what, even though I don't really know who the real "me" is right now. I know that in the process of actually practicing being myself I will find out who I really am. I now accept myself as myself and for myself and that is completely okay. I am going to be who I am and if others don't like me the way I really am, well, that will be their choice and I do not have to spend any amount of time trying to change the way that others feel about me. I do not have to take it personally because I will know that it's not about me anyway... I am fine just the way I am and I am happy with the way I am. I will handle whatever happens when I get off the bus in Phoenix from a place of, "How I handle this is completely up to me and how I choose to handle it. How do I want to handle it?" And THAT will come from an even deeper place of, "It's okay for me to be happy. It's okay for me to make choices that are based on what will make me happy. It's okay for me to trust myself and the way I feel about things."

That night was an amazing experience for me. That night I went through a process of learning that I was really okay and that I could trust myself. That night I broke the pattern of my conditioning. That night I chose to be free.

When Cynthia woke up on Tuesday morning we continued our conversation from the previous day. And I soaked it all in and hung onto everything I learned so that I would have it to apply to my own life.

Our bus pulled into the station in L.A. in the early afternoon and that was the last time I saw Cynthia. I was sorry to see her go, but I was so grateful for the day that I had experienced with her because now I felt as if I actually had a real chance to make a good life for myself.

In Los Angeles we were supposed to have a two-hour layover, which turned into about a 3½ hour layover. *That* was my first opportunity to use some of the stuff I was in the process of learning. For me, that was an extremely interesting 3½ hours. I say, "for me," because for someone just looking on, it would not have seemed in any way remarkable. But for me that experience was huge because twenty-four hours previous to this, it would have been a very different experience from the one I created for myself.

There were any number of things during that layover that I could have—and previously would have—chosen to be upset about. Here are a few of them:

- That bus station is enormous, and it was so crowded with people that there were no seats to sit in and a limited amount of floor space to sit on.
- There were little kids running around pretty much out of control and making a LOT of noise.
- I had to sit on the floor for hours to save my place in line.
- My stuff had to be guarded at all times or it could have easily walked away.

- The restroom was gross.
- The ATM would not work for me.

I could go on and on. If you are looking for negative things to experience you can *always* find them.

This seemed like a good place for me to start using the stuff that I was in the process of learning, so I deliberately noticed several things that I could be upset about if I chose to. And then I deliberately looked for aspects of those things that I could appreciate.

- The restroom was gross, but at least there was a restroom available.
- The kids running around were noisy, yes, but they were making fun noise instead of obnoxious noise. I love to hear children laughing.
- So what if I had to sit on the floor? I was pretty close to the beginning of the line, so that meant I would be able to get a good window seat on the bus when we were finally allowed to board.
- The people sitting around me were *very* interesting to observe. (A bus station is a great place to people-watch!)
- The ATM did not work, but that was actually a good thing because if I had been able to withdraw money, my checking account would have been seriously overdrawn and that would have been one more thing I would have to worry about.

Probably the most positive thing I found was the opportunity to practice being myself in a situation where I normally would have just kept my mouth shut and felt sorry for myself.

I found myself looking for the happiness inside me that I knew was there. And it was a wonderful thing that even in a situation like that, where most people would not think to deliberately choose to be positive, I was able to actually find feelings of happiness.

If you are looking for positive things to experience you can *always* find them! And sitting there on the floor of the Greyhound station in Los Angeles, California I looked for positive things to experience — and I found them! And in deliberately looking for positive things to experience, I found happiness inside myself.

It was from *that* place that I began practicing being myself. It was amazing! I actually *started* conversations with the people around me! And I even looked them in the face while I was doing it! And they were nice to me! They even seemed to appreciate someone striking up a conversation with them first! They didn't think I was stupid or boring. They were just happy to have a conversation going to help pass the time in a pleasant way. It was very uncomfortable, but I did it anyway, and as I did so I knew I would never be the same.

From that place of happiness inside myself I looked around that bus station and I saw how hard the Greyhound employees were working to make things as easy on their customers as possible. And I let them know that I appreciated it. And I felt wonderful because those people usually only get complaints. It was a great feeling to help someone else to have a better day.

I practiced and I practiced and I practiced. And yes, I did have to make myself take those first steps (*"I see you Fear. I know what you want. You have no power over me."*), but I found that once those steps were taken things flowed along nicely. And I was honestly enjoying myself. I can't tell you what that meant to me. It was like I was watching from outside myself and asking, "Who is that woman? She is relaxed and smiling and taking one thing at a time instead of making things hard on herself by worrying about what the others think of her or stressing out about what's going to happen later. Could that really be me? Could it really be this easy? This feels really good!"

Sitting on the floor of the bus station in L.A., I continued to learn things that contributed to the wonderful shift in my experience of my life that happened when I came to Arizona.

Sitting on the floor of that bus station I learned that not only do I like feeling good, but that allowing myself to feel good is a lot easier on me than *not* feeling good, because it is so much more enjoyable!

So you may be wondering, "Can it really be that easy?" And my answer is absolutely, "Yes!" The most difficult thing about it is getting yourself to remember. It is now years later and I still find myself in people-pleaser mode every once in a while. Not nearly so often, though. But that—remembering—was the most difficult thing about this whole process. It's really easy to stay in your comfort zone, even if your comfort zone is a place of victimhood and unhappiness. It would be easy to leave your car stuck in the mud, but if you did that, you'd have to stay stuck in the mud! I could have easily fallen back into my old patterns, but I knew that if I did that it wouldn't be long before I ended up right back in Portland—right back in the mud.

This is what I learned during the process of breaking free of my "conditioning": There is no growth in my comfort zone! If I wanted my life to change, then I had to be the one to change my life. And if I wanted to change my life, I had to be the one to change!

During this process—at the bus station in L.A. and then back on the bus and into Phoenix—I practiced going outside my comfort zone. I practiced finding beauty wherever I looked. I practiced talking to people I didn't know and not worrying about whether or not they thought I was stupid. I practiced thinking positive thoughts and looking for things to be grateful for. And during all of this I learned that I could make it really hard work, or I could have fun with it. However I chose to handle it would be up to me. I did try it both ways and I'll tell you this—hard work (struggle) is no fun!

I tried forcing it, which was not only exhausting, but it felt completely phony and forced. There is no joy in struggle. Have you ever tried to force something to be a certain way? And doesn't that just feel unnatural? There is far more power (and joy!) in relaxing and going with the flow of things—taking them as they come and handling them however you choose to handle them in the moment—than there is in trying to use force. Try it for yourself and you will see what I mean. It's just a matter of how you look at things—it's all about perspective.

I found that if I looked at things as if I had to struggle my way through, or as if I had to "overcome" them, I created a lot of hard work for myself. It was like trying to climb up the sheer face of a cliff. It was almost impossible to keep a good grip and I was terrified that I'd get halfway up and then fall. And if I fell this time I knew it was just a matter of time before I would be dead.

I knew there had to be another way. At this point I could tell that I was making things far more difficult for myself than they really needed to be. I knew I was needlessly stressing myself out, so I opened *Building Your Field of Dreams* just to try to take my mind off of my mountain climbing exercise. This is what my eyes were drawn to when I just let the book fall open, "...if you were starting fresh with a no-limits attitude, what would you do?" Boy, did THAT give me something to think about!

If I were starting fresh, with a "no-limits" attitude, what would I do? How would I handle things if I *knew* I could handle anything?

- Well, first I would just plain relax! I would remember to breathe and I would relax my jaw, neck, and shoulders.
- I would take things one thing at a time, in the moment. After all, isn't "now" all we really have?
- And then I would relax!
- I would ask myself, "What do I really want in this moment?" And I would start there.
- And then I would remind myself to breathe and bring my shoulders back down where they belong, instead of up around my ears.
- I would remember that I know that the universe is friendly and on my side. And if the universe is friendly and wants me to do well, how can there be any limits to what I can accomplish?
- Oh yeah, and then I would remember to relax.
- And then I would begin to make choices that felt right for me, instead of making choices out of desperation or out of a need for validation from someone else.
- I would practice trusting the God that I was coming to believe in.
- And I would practice trusting my Self.
- I would remind myself to relax and to breathe.
- I would allow myself to actually enjoy being in the middle of whatever I happened to be experiencing in the moment that I was in.

- If I were starting fresh, with a "no-limits" attitude, I would practice looking at my life as if it were an adventure instead of something I needed to survive or "overcome" or "make it through".

This was a new concept for me, and it was a biggie. I had taken a leap of Faith in getting on that bus — now was not the time to give up! I hadn't even arrived in Phoenix yet. I knew that if I was going to make it in an unfamiliar city I was going to have to learn to do things very differently from the way I had always done things. I needed to learn to make my choices and live my life from a place of knowing that God loves me and wants me to do well, instead of from a place of Fear and, "I know I'll never be happy, so why should I even try."

So, between L.A. and Phoenix, I practiced and I practiced and I reminded myself over and over and over that how I deal with the things that come up in my life can only be ultimately and completely up to me. No other person on this planet is responsible for the choices that I make. I am responsible for how I look at things, how I handle things, and my *experience* of things. If I could look at everything that came up from a place of "there are no limits to what I can accomplish" then the possibilities of the things I could potentially accomplish were endless, weren't they? How exciting!

From L.A. to Phoenix, I concentrated on Spirit and my connection to Spirit. There's a saying that goes like this: "If you're not feeling close to God, who moved?" If you pay attention to how you feel, you will know whether or not you are pinching yourself off from Spirit. Spirit is always there and available to us, but we have to allow *ourselves* to be available to receive the connection that provides us with the positive, "no-limits" stuff that I was in the process of learning.

I found that my connection to Spirit felt the strongest when I deliberately chose to trust the process of what I was experiencing right then.

"Our doubts are traitors, and make us lose the good we oft might win – by fearing to attempt."

And

"Where I place my attention, I am placing my intention."

And

"My history need not determine my destiny."

And all the other quotes I had stuck in my back pocket were the tools that I used to keep myself focused on what I wanted to accomplish.

What would happen to me if I allowed my doubts to dominate my thoughts?

Where am I placing my attention moment to moment?

Just because I have a history of being a victim... does that mean I am *meant* to live my life as a victim? No. Not at all. Only if I choose to go back to looking at my life that way.

I spent the hours between L.A. and Phoenix practicing looking for things to be grateful for, practicing looking for positive thoughts, and practicing creating a happy future for myself in my mind. And when the bus pulled into the station in Phoenix, I stepped off of it with a feeling of adventure and a smile on my face. In my previous life I would have stepped off that bus with feelings of resignation and fear. I would have been crying and wondering, "What am I going to do now?" "What's going to happen to me?" "Oh, my God, what have I done?!"

But not now. I had learned so much during the past two days—I was a completely different person. I could never go back to being the mousy little victim who had climbed the steps of that bus in Portland. I felt ready for anything…

Pop Your Paradigm!

Chapter 7

A Brand New Me

"This above all: To thine own self be true"
~ William Shakespeare

It has now been a lot of years since I stepped off that Greyhound bus in Phoenix, Arizona. I can't help but feel a sense of celebration not only because I am still alive, but because I'm living a rich, wonderful life of Love and Joy. Has it really been that long since I was sitting on that bus talking with and learning so much from Cynthia? Sometimes it feels like I've been here forever, and sometimes it feels like that intense period of my life was just yesterday. But I always look back on that time with a sense of awe both because of all the things I learned at once and because *I made it!* I not only survived, but I was successful in creating not just a whole new life for myself, but a whole new *way of living*.

The bus pulled into the Greyhound station at 24th Street and Buckeye in Phoenix at about 11:50 p.m. on Tuesday June 27, 2000. I had trouble believing how wonderful I felt. I had no idea whether Jeff would be there waiting for me or not. I hadn't slept since the previous Saturday night. I had barely eaten during those two days. I had no idea what I was going to have to do to be able to make it in Phoenix. But even with all of that, I felt wonderful, hopeful, and more *alive* than I had ever felt before.

I remember thinking as I left Portland that I felt as if I were jumping off a cliff—I felt as if I were taking a giant and complete leap of Faith, and that I was just going to have to trust that I would grow some wings on my way down so I would be able to land myself safely. And here I was, just getting ready to hit the ground, and I felt like I was going to do it without breaking any bones! Is this what people mean when they say, "He (or she) hit the ground running?" Well, I didn't necessarily feel like I was running, but I did not feel like I was hurting, either. I actually felt happy to be alive, which was definitely not a normal feeling for me.

As I stood up and took my backpack down from the overhead compartment I actually had a smile on my face! And do you want to know why? It was because I had surrendered any and all expectations—good or bad. I had decided to just plain place my faith in a friendly universe and treat this whole situation like a great adventure. I figured it was either that or suffer a nervous breakdown. I decided I might as well have as much fun as I could with whatever showed up. Why not?

So that was how I was able to have a real smile (instead of a forced, "grit your teeth and get through this as best you can" smile) on my face as I took those steps off the bus and forward into a new life.

I felt like a completely different person from the one who had climbed up those steps the previous day. I *was* (I *am*) completely different. I may still be in the same physical body, have the same name, same parents, same children, same history — but in changing my way of thinking and looking at things, I absolutely changed how I experience my life!

I walked down those steps with my head up, a smile on my face, a sense of adventure, complete faith in the possibility of a wonderful new life for myself, and — incredibly — a completely unfamiliar feeling of trust in myself and my decision making abilities. I had decided that I was going to be true to myself, even though I didn't know what that really meant. But I was willing to find out. I was willing to try trusting my intuition and making my decisions from there. I was willing to check in with my gut — and trust what it told me — before making any decision or taking any action. THAT was the adventure!

In *Building Your Field of Dreams* Mary says, "Go to the edge of the light you see." That is the same thing as, "Take the first step in faith." Same principle, different way of looking at it. I recently heard Jack Canfield say it something like this: "When you're driving at night, your headlights only shine ahead of you about 200 feet, but you can drive the entire distance from California to New York at night, with just the next 200 feet illuminated. You don't have to be able to see any farther ahead than that to be able to successfully drive from one side of America to the other." And even driving during the day, you can only see so far ahead of you. You don't have to see the whole staircase. You can Trust.

As I stepped off of that bus, and the heat landed on me like a giant invisible blanket, I felt a complete sense of trust that I was doing the right thing for myself. *(But, my God! How am I going to be able to bear this heat?! I can't breathe!)*

I walked into the building (*Thank you, God, for air conditioning!*) and immediately looked around to make sure that Jeff wasn't there waiting for me. He wasn't in the building, so I went out to the parking lot to make sure he wasn't out there in his truck. He wasn't there either. I think a part of me was kind of disappointed that he wasn't there. I was feeling very sure of myself (cocky) and was sort of looking forward to demonstrating my newfound independence and inner strength to him (and to myself) by telling him to go away.

Ha! If he had been there my "newfound independence and inner strength" probably would have instantly self-destructed and I would have found myself on my way back to Portland in a heartbeat. My lifelong conditioning and habits of thinking would have kicked right back in like I had never discovered any other way of being.

But I had been right about one thing. The universe really is friendly and on my side. So Jeff was NOT there when I got off the bus, which left me free to practice making good, healthy choices for myself just because the situation I found myself in was completely different from any other situation I had ever experienced in my life.

I did find myself struggling, though, with the fear that continually showed up and threatened to cut off my supply of oxygen. Throughout this whole experience I went back and forth between fear and faith. One minute I would be petrified because the steps I was taking were so huge and I really had no clue what I was going to do. And the next minute I would remember the decisions I had made during my bus ride. It was really difficult, but whenever I would find myself in that place of fear (I was petrified) I would remind myself of all that I had learned so far. I would remind (re-mind) myself that I live in a friendly universe. I would remind myself that I did not have to give in to my fear. I did not have to let my fear dictate what my actions would be. I would remind myself that I had decided to trust my intuition and take things one step (in faith) at a time. Whenever my fear would get in my face and scream at me,

> *Just look at what you've gotten yourself into NOW! You are stuck at the Greyhound station in Phoenix and you have no clue what you're going to do next. You are so stupid! You know you're not going to be able to make it on your own here — why did you do this to yourself?! You jumped into this river and you don't even know how to swim! Who's going to save you from drowning? How are you going to survive? I can't believe the things you do to yourself sometimes! And this is a biggie, isn't it? You know you could die here, don't you? How are you going to keep yourself alive? You think you're going to be able to start a whole new life here? Ha! Dream on, sister! You are so screwed! You might as well call Jeff now and have him rescue you. You know you're going to end up doing that sooner or later, and the longer you wait the angrier he's going to be and the worse your punishment will be. You might as well get it over with now and save yourself the pain of this attempt to gain your freedom. You are never going to succeed at this and you know it. Give up now, would you? I want to go home where I can breathe and where I am comfortable and where I have at least some idea of what's going to happen next!*

I would look at that fear and listen to it for a while. And then I would decide not to let it have the power to stop me.

> *I see you Fear. I know what you want. Thanks for sharing your opinion. I appreciate that you're just trying to protect me, but you're not going to make me change my mind. You have no power over me so back off, sit down and shut up, please and thank you!*

It was really hard, but I did it. In fact I did it over and over and over again. And again. And then again.

There were a couple of other things that popped up often during this time: anger and blame. They were both ugly and very, very insistent. I had to really concentrate on not giving in and letting them have their way with me. This is a little of what that looked like:

> *It's all HIS fault that I'm here. If he had just left me alone I wouldn't be in this position now. Just look at where I am. I had no choice but to run away and now I'm in this place where it's hard for me to breathe because it's so hot. There are homeless people all over the place. And – oh yeah – that includes me. I am now homeless and living at the Greyhound station in Phoenix and it's all his fault. I have landed in Hell and HE is to blame! Why couldn't he have just been nice? Why couldn't he have just been what I wanted him to be? The whole reason I'm here is because he can't let go of his bitterness and anger. Why do I always have to be a victim? Why couldn't he just love me like he said he did? Now, here I am – no job, no money, no place to go – and he's to blame because he always chose to be mean and treat me like shit…*

And on and on, around and around the circle of bitterness, anger, and blame.

I could have gone to that place of anger and blame and stayed, and on any normal day in my life that would have been right where I would have pitched my tent and lived for a while. But this day was far from *normal*, thank God!

When I got off that bus it was with the deliberate intention of creating a whole new, positive life for myself — not to continue doing what I had always done, which would have gotten me what I had always gotten. I knew that if I looked at my life in Phoenix from a place of, "This is horrible and it's all his fault." I would have ended up in a, "This is horrible..." kind of place. I did not want that! I did not want to create another version of the same kind of life I had always experienced! And my new life had to start with the choices that I was making from *this point!* If I wanted to shift my direction and go down the road I wanted to go down, then I needed to take responsibility for which way I turned my steering wheel *in this moment*, didn't I?

> *So what should I do? Should I look at it from a place of, "This is horrible and it's all MY fault!"? Well, I guess I could. It's not like I haven't done THAT before, either, now is it? And did it serve me to blame myself? No. All that ever did was add to my feelings of dislike for myself. And how positive is that? Not! Okay, so what's the most positive way I can find of looking at the situation I now find myself in? It is not Jeff's fault that I am homeless in the bus station in Phoenix. It was my choice to come here. Does that mean I am to blame? Why does anybody have to be at fault? What good is it going to do me to place blame? It won't help the situation and it won't make me feel better. If I concentrate on placing blame won't that just put me right back in*

the position of being a victim? If I concentrate on placing blame, isn't that the same thing as me handing my power right back over to him? Oh wow! I don't EVEN want to go back to THAT place! All right then, how should I look at this? How about this: This is where I am. This IS the situation I am in. What I choose to do with it is completely up to me. My power is in the choice that I make right now. I am where I am and it is what it is and my choice will be my choice and what comes as a result of my choice will be what comes as the result of my choice. And from that place I will be able to make another choice. My power is in right now, and what I do with right now and how I look at right now is completely up to me! It has nothing to do with him. He is wherever he is. And I am where I am and what I choose to do with where I am will determine where I will be in an hour or a day or a week.

Sitting here at my computer, in my office, in the home that I share with my husband, Rick, I can't help but be amazed at where I have ended up as a result of the choices that I made all those years ago at the Greyhound station in Phoenix, Arizona.

The universe truly is friendly — you just have to be willing to see it that way if you want to experience it that way. Over the next few hours, days, and weeks I continually reminded myself that the road I went down was completely up to me. How I looked at and experienced things that happened was completely up to me. (I know, I'm repeating myself. I'm doing that on purpose, because that was what I had to do then. I had to continually remind myself of these things because I was in the process of breaking a pattern that I had lived for thirty-five years! I had to practice and practice and practice my new way of thinking and looking at things.) I kept reminding myself that I was responsible for my choices and actions and—ultimately—my own happiness. If I had known then what I know now, I wouldn't have even bothered using the word "happiness"—I would have gone straight to the word "Joy"...

So it's wonderful to look back from where I am now, because I know how it all turned out. At the time, though, it took an incredible amount of determination and strength to keep my chin up and not fall right back into being a victim. The Greyhound station in Phoenix could be a very scary place for a woman alone in the middle of the night, and I had a very hard time keeping myself from seeing it that way. For the most part I was successful—I just tried to concentrate on other things, on things that I could be grateful for... Things like air conditioning, bottled water, and hamburgers!

The first thing I needed to do (after getting something in my stomach) was check my voice mail. I really needed to know what Jeff was up to—whether he was in Phoenix, on his way to Phoenix, or sitting in Portland being pitiful and/or angry. I would be able to tell what was up with him by the voice mail he had left during the two days I had been on the bus. My problem, though, was the amount of money it would cost me to check twenty minutes (at least) worth of messages on a Portland number while roaming in Phoenix. I could just see my bill being way more money than I wanted to be responsible for. No thanks. So what could I do about this? Well, the plan was to start a whole new life in Arizona—so why not start at the beginning with an Arizona phone number?

I knew that Verizon Wireless has 24-hour customer service, and they also have an 800 number that wouldn't cost me anything from a pay phone. So I called them right then. (It wasn't like I had anything better to do, you know?) I asked the Customer Service Representative if my voice mail would transfer over along with the new number. She assured me that it would, and so I went ahead and switched to an Arizona number. It was quick and painless. I had always appreciated Verizon Wireless for their wonderful customer service and how on top of things they are whenever I need to call them, and this was no exception.

So my Oregon number was disconnected and my Arizona number was activated just like that. Unfortunately for me at the time, my voice mail did NOT transfer over with the number. My voice mail — my only way of monitoring what Jeff was doing, which meant my only way of knowing whether or not I needed to be terrified that he might show up — was lost and gone forever the second that Oregon number was disconnected. I know this because I called Verizon back and they searched and searched the system for me and they couldn't find it anywhere. I stood in the middle of that bus station and I cussed. For about ninety seconds I was *furious!* So much for my appreciation for Verizon Wireless and them being on top of things! This was stuff that I *needed* to know — stuff I had *depended* on being able to find out and base my decisions on — and now it was gone forever and I was left standing there with my backpack and my duffel bag and my cell phone with a new number and NO WAY of knowing if he was going to walk up behind me sometime that night and punch me in the head. I was unbelievably frustrated. Okay, I was just plain pissed.

And I was so tired. I cannot even begin to describe how exhausted I was, both physically and emotionally. I just wanted to lie down somewhere and go to sleep.

And there I was in the bus station. There were other people there who didn't seem to have a problem sleeping in the bus station. There were people sleeping on the floor and in chairs—why couldn't I do that, too? Well, in the first place, the things I had with me were all things that I would need, and if I went to sleep my bags might walk away. And in the second place, since I had no idea what Jeff was up to there was no way in hell I was going to close my eyes even for a second! Yep—I was pissed and I was frustrated and I just wanted to sit down someplace and cry.

This seemed like a great time to pull my quotes out of my back pocket because I actually (miracle of miracles!) recognized that I was feeling stuck in my frustration. I knew that if I didn't do something to get myself out of that stuck feeling, no ideas about what I could do to make things better were going to show up because I just plain wasn't open to it. So I reached into my back pocket for my quotes, and guess who I found in my hot little hand! It was none other than Mr. Einstein telling me, "The significant problems we face cannot be solved at the level of thinking that created them." That was unbelievably appropriate to the situation, wasn't it? When I read it I was brought up short. What was I standing there doing? Once again, I was creating a problem where no problem actually existed, just because I was standing there worrying about what *might* happen. I was wasting my time and energy on "What if…" instead of focusing on what was going on in the "now" and dealing with that. In worrying about Jeff *maybe* showing up, I wasn't leaving myself any room to handle the things I needed to focus on in that moment. I needed to get off the problem level and start being open to solutions or I was going to be paralyzed right there in the bus station, unable to move forward and unwilling to go back. That was not acceptable to me. So I stood there with Albert Einstein in my hand and I took that as a message that I needed to let go of worrying about whether or not Jeff was going to show up. If he ever *did* show up, I would deal with it then. In the meantime, I had more immediate things to focus on. So it was with huge effort and an incredible amount of determination (which I had no idea I had in me) that I made myself (over and over again) let go of the worry that Jeff *might* show up in Phoenix.

So unfortunately, (or maybe I should say "fortunately." I actually came to feel blessed by that situation later.) there was nothing I could do about the voice mail situation. But I could do something about getting some sleep. I picked up the phone again and started calling motels. I knew I needed to get some sleep before I tried making any decisions about what to do next. It was now the early morning hours of Wednesday, June 28th, and the last sleep I gotten had been the previous Saturday night. I was completely exhausted. I needed to sleep, and I needed to do it soon or I was going to collapse, and then what would become of me?

The cheapest room I could find that had a shuttle that would come and pick me up was $54.00. God that seemed like a lot of money! Especially since I now had less than $80 to my name. I was regretting the burger I had eaten earlier…

But I had to do what I had to do, right? And where was my Faith? Had I lost it already? I was shocked to realize that I really *hadn't* lost my Faith. It was still there with me and it still felt strong and true. I still felt as if I was doing the right thing for myself. I had never felt this good about myself before in my life and it was a wonderful—if somewhat alien—feeling.

But I was so tired and there was the very real fact that if I wanted to sleep I was going to have to spend $54.00 of the money that I had left. That was going to leave me with less than $20.00. Scary…

The other problem with getting that room was that they had no vacancies right then. The guy I spoke with told me to call back at 8:00 in the morning — maybe they would have something then. I was *SO* frustrated! 8:00 was seven hours away and I was just so tired…

There were so many incredible blessings in this whole situation. Just as my learning experience during the trip from Portland had been intense, my night spent at the bus station in Phoenix was equally intense. During that night I found out what I could be made of if I would just allow myself to trust myself to do what felt right.

For seven hours I hung out at the bus station. I tried to read, but I was too tired to concentrate. I watched the people — that was interesting for a while. I thought long and hard about what I wanted for myself in general. And, in general, what I wanted for myself was this: I wanted to feel safe in my own life, and I wanted to find out what it meant to really "be happy." That was what I wanted, and I was willing to do whatever I needed to do to create that life for myself.

Well, that was all fine and dandy to contemplate and dream about, but in that moment I was falling asleep and that was not a good thing. I seriously felt that I could not afford to fall asleep in the middle of the bus station. I decided I needed to get up and move around. So I transferred myself and my bags out to the front of the station for a while, just for something different and (hopefully) more interesting — something that would help me stay awake. Boy, was I ever right about that! The front entrance of the bus station is where the *really* interesting people hang out.

There were a couple of taxi drivers who seemed like decent enough guys if I just ignored the fact that they both insisted that I was not going to find a good life in Arizona. They insisted on telling me all of the negative things they could think of about Phoenix. I think they meant well, and I appreciated that, but it did take some effort not to get discouraged. It was a good test of the strength of my decision to look for positives, and it was a wonderful feeling to discover that even in that situation and atmosphere of negativity I was able to stay in a positive frame of mind. I found that the more I consciously stayed there in that positive frame of mind, the easier it was for me to actually *stay* there. My discoveries on the bus about being able to see things however I *chose* to see things really served me well through that whole night. I did not have to go to a place of negativity if I didn't want to go there. And I chose not to go there, and I felt a sense of power in myself that I had never known was there and that I never would have discovered if I had not run away from Portland. Through that night I proved to myself over and over again that circumstances outside myself did not have to determine how I felt on the *inside*.

There were quite a few people out there, but only two others besides the taxi drivers that I remember clearly. The rest of them either didn't have anything to say, or they weren't out there for very long.

There was a guy who was probably in his mid-twenties. I think his name was Pete. I don't remember where he was coming from, but I do remember that he had just arrived in Phoenix and he was trying to figure out how he was going to get the rest of the way home. He lived sixty miles away and he said there was no one he could call. He had run out of money, so he was stuck there at the Greyhound station until he figured something out for himself. He had a very positive attitude about his situation. He just knew that the solution to his problem would show up and in the meantime he was just hanging out with us. I was impressed. What a coincidence, huh? I had just recently decided to look at things in that way, and who do I run into but someone who looked at things that way! He just knew that he'd be okay and that his answer would show up whenever it showed up.

And there was a young woman who said her name was Michelle. She was probably about twenty years old and she was very pretty. She was also very angry. Her anger was not apparent at first. It was only when I got into a real conversation with her that I got the sense that she was an extremely angry young lady. Her "friends" had dropped her off at the bus station hours before I met her. They had promised to bring her back enough money to get her home to New York and then she had never seen them again. She had tried calling them, but they would not answer their phone. It seemed that they had just dumped her off and left her to her own devices at the bus station.

When I first went outside I just leaned against a pillar and observed what was going on out there.

And I sweated. I had never in my life experienced such heat outdoors in the middle of the night. It was weird and it was uncomfortable. But I decided to deal with it for a while before I went back in.

I leaned and I sweated (like a horse!) and I watched and I listened. I watched people come and go. I watched the people who were hanging out. I listened to the conversations that were going on. It was pretty lively out there.

One of the taxi drivers drew me into their conversation. He wanted to know all about me and why I was there. I told him some of my story and that was when the two of them started talking about how they thought I had made a bad decision in coming to Phoenix. They said that this was a terrible place to start over. They did give a lot of reasons why, but I deliberately chose to disregard all of the negative things they told me. I did not want to start out focusing on negatives. If I did that I would be discouraged right from the start and I would end up making decisions based on that. I did not want that to be my starting point. I wanted to start fresh, with a positive outlook, and I wanted to continue looking for solutions to my current problems. I did not want to have even more problems dumped on me, so I just didn't acknowledge the things they told me. And in fact they were just telling me their perceptions, weren't they? I wanted to decide for myself what I liked or didn't like. They were very nice guys and I do believe they meant well, and I really appreciated that, so that was what I focused on.

The hours passed and as I tried to get used to the heat I chatted with the others. One of the taxi drivers got a fare and he left. The other one was still there and I was talking with him and Pete and Michelle. It was about 3:30 in the morning when a car pulled up right in front of us and an extremely upset young lady jumped out of it, walked up to Pete, and said, "Do you want a car? I'll sign it over to you right now."

He immediately said, "Yeah! I do! Are you really giving your car away?"

"Yes! I've had it with my boyfriend hitting me! My mom got me a bus ticket so I can get home, and she said I should just sign my car over to someone at the bus station. So that's what I'm doing!"

It was very cool to witness. She dug through the trash in the car, found the title and signed it, handed him the key, and said, "Here you go. Sorry about the mess!"

She then ran into the building as if there was a monster chasing her. That young woman was terrified and I completely understood how she felt, having been in almost the exact same place not two days before!

I was kind of frustrated, though, that she hadn't asked *me* if I wanted the car. After all, I really needed it. My situation so closely paralleled hers that I couldn't help thinking that it really would have been something if she had walked up to me instead of him.

On the other hand, it was awesome to watch that young man's faith pay off in such a huge way. He had just known that he would find a way to get himself that last sixty miles home. He didn't know how it would happen, and he didn't try to control how it would happen. He just knew it would happen for him. And it did happen for him in a way that nobody ever could have predicted. But he never focused on the problem. He acknowledged the facts: he was sixty miles from home, there was no one he could call to come and get him, and he had no money to get himself there. And then he kept himself open for a solution, and that solution presented itself right out of the blue. It was a wonderful thing to witness, and it added to my own faith that good things could happen for me if I allowed them to. While watching that happen for him, I felt as if the universe was confirming for me that I was on the right track in changing my way of handling things.

Yes, I continued to be frustrated for a while, and I was very envious as I watched him happily hop in the car and drive away. But eventually I was able to let that go and I decided that it was probably for the best that he found his solution and I was not going to end up living in a car in an unfamiliar city. Hindsight has definitely shown me that having that car handed to me would *not* have been the best thing for me and my situation.

So after we all watched him drive away with our mouths hanging open because it all happened so fast, it was me, Michelle, and the other taxi driver left. The taxi driver got a fare right away and then it was just us girls.

Michelle and I chatted, and after a while the subject turned to our respective situations. It was 4:00 in the morning and she was still insisting that her friends were going to show up with some money for her. They had dropped her off at about 7:00 the previous evening and they still weren't answering their phone. But she was still counting on them coming back. It looked to me like she was stuck in a place of wishful thinking, probably because she didn't want to face the fact that she was going to have to figure something out on her own.

She knew my situation because she had been listening to my earlier conversation with the taxi drivers. She suggested to me that she and I should rent a room together. She knew where we could get a (supposedly) decent one for about $75.00 per week.

Now in my previous life I would have ignored the things that my intuition was screaming at me. *(Don't you dare give up the last of your money to pay for a room to share with this person that you don't know — and that you don't trust! You can tell by the way you feel that this is not what you really want to do! So don't do it!)* I would have ignored all that in favor of jumping on what seemed like an easy solution to my current predicament. Not this time. This time I decided to trust what my gut was telling me. I said, "No thanks. I need to figure this out on my own." Saying no was a new thing for me. It felt weird and I felt bad for her. On the other hand it felt good to actually trust my own feelings and not give in, either to the people-pleaser in me who did not want to be responsible for hurting someone else's feelings, or to the part of me that usually tried to find the easy way out whether it was healthy for me or not.

Well, my saying "no thanks" did not stop her from trying to convince me to do it. She had all sorts of reasons why I should just go ahead and do what she wanted me to do. She said that if I would just pay for the room, she would pay me back for half of the cost. She insisted that she would be able to get the money to accomplish this from her friends that had dropped her off at the bus station. She honestly didn't understand my skepticism about that. She pointed out that the sooner I had a place to stay, the easier it would be for me to get a job and get on my feet. And if she could stay with me, she would be able to do the same. I had red flags popping up all over the place and sirens going off big time in the back of my mind. *(Don't you dare give in to her! Don't you dare let her talk you into this! You know it would be a huge mistake! Don't do it. There's another way. You may not know what it is right now, but you know there's a better way than placing your trust in this person.)*

As I continued to decline, she became more and more insistent. And then she did something that I will never understand. I did not understand the point of it then, and I don't understand it now. She completely sabotaged herself without realizing that was what she was doing. I don't know why, but it was then that she informed me that she had been lying to me about her name. The only thing I can think of is that she was attempting to gain my trust by coming clean. She told me that her name really wasn't Michelle. Her name was really April. She pulled out her ID card to prove it to me. It wasn't that big of a deal to me. This was just proof that I was right not to trust her, because if she would lie about that, what else would she lie about? She was frantic to prove to me what her real name was, so I looked at her card and in my mind I sent a huge "Thank you" to my intuition. The longer I sat there and talked to that young woman, the weirder that whole situation seemed to me.

The conversation went from her just trying to coax me into paying for a room for a week, to tears on her part because of her bad situation, to her trying to make me feel responsible for rescuing her from her situation. ("These are all the bad things that are going to happen to me if you don't do what I want you to do.") I finally got tired of listening to her and told her I'd talk to her later. And then I made my escape back into the building.

> *Don't you go feeling guilty now! You know you don't want to go where that road will take you. Trust yourself! You can see where you will end up if you let her make you feel guilty enough to do what she wants. This is a perfect opportunity for you to practice making a healthy choice for yourself. You are not responsible for her feelings and if you feel guilty that is completely your choice. You need to do what's right for you, and you know that falling in with that young woman would be a huge mistake. Let her be responsible for her own stuff. And you be responsible for yours.*

Logic said that getting a room for a whole week with $75 (which was almost all the money I had left) made a lot more sense than spending $54 on one night in a motel. But I decided to trust my feelings about that. My gut feelings screamed at me whenever I seriously considered the weekly room. I could have found out from her where that room was and just rented it for myself, but every time I seriously considered doing that it just felt *wrong*.

So I did what I had decided on the bus that I was going to do. I trusted myself and my judgment. I made a choice and I took complete responsibility for making that choice. And I felt good. I could hear Mary Morrissey in the back of my mind saying, "Go to the edge of the light that you see." And that's what I did. I surrendered to what felt right to me, even though logic said it didn't make sense. I left Michelle/April outside and I went into the air conditioned building and I bought a cup of coffee to help me stay awake and I watched TV for the next three hours.

And promptly at 8:00 I called that motel. The guy that I had spoken with the night before had been right and they did have a vacant room for me. As soon as I called, they had a shuttle on its way to pick me up.

As I waited for it to arrive, I had visions of laying my head down and getting some real sleep, rather than just dozing here and there like I had been doing for four days straight. Just the thought of that felt like heaven!

Ten minutes later I was climbing up the steps into the shuttle, happily leaving that Greyhound station in my history.

Chapter 8

Hello, New Life!

*"Go where you want to go
Do what you want to do
Be who you want to be
In Freedom and Joy!"
~ Francine Jarry*

As the shuttle pulled away from the Greyhound station and I got to look around in the daylight I couldn't help but wonder how Phoenix and Portland could be on the same planet, much less in the same country. There is not much in Phoenix that is like anything in Portland. The buildings are different. The landscape is different. The climate is different. The very quality of the air is different. I looked out the windows of that shuttle and I felt as if I were an alien who had just landed on this planet and who had no idea what to do with all the unfamiliar, but strangely familiar, things that I was seeing. What I mean is, the freeways were freeways, but they didn't look much like the freeways in Oregon. The buildings were buildings, but they didn't look much like the buildings in Oregon. The air was breathable, but other than that it wasn't much like the air in Oregon. And it was bright! The sun was reflecting off of absolutely everything and I had a really hard time with it. I was uncomfortable—in fact, I was completely out of both my element *and* my comfort zone!

I remember looking out those shuttle windows and feeling completely lost, indescribably lonely, absolutely exhausted, and not sure I was going to make it.

And then, thank God, there was the part of me that was still looking for the sense of adventure in my situation. It was kind of back behind all the other feelings that I was experiencing right then, but it was *there,* and that was a wonderful thing—it was like a flotation device I was clinging to, to keep myself from drowning in all that other stuff that could have so easily sucked me in if I didn't stay above it.

As I got out of the shuttle and walked into the motel I was just concentrating on staying upright. I was so tired!

The man behind the counter, Jim, was so kind to me. I stood there as I was checking in and suddenly, out of nowhere, I just burst into tears. Why? It was because I had forgotten to bring my toothbrush when I left Portland. I had remembered everything else but that. And now I was so anticipating taking a shower and feeling clean again after so long—and after sweating so much the during the night—that I could only think of how unfinished that would seem if I couldn't get my teeth brushed, too. Silly, I know. And I knew at the time how silly I was being, but at that point I just couldn't help it. The dam just happened to burst right there in the lobby of that motel.

I have learned to believe that everything happens for a reason, and I do not believe that there is any such thing as coincidence. What happened next was something that served to convince me of both of these things.

I could not have known this because I hadn't had a lot of experience with motels, but they had a pile of brand new toothbrushes and little tubes of toothpaste in their back office. I had no way of knowing that, and so I never would have thought to ask about it. If I hadn't burst into tears and blurted it out that I didn't even have a toothbrush, I would have continued to be without a toothbrush.

I know, it was a really small thing. But for me it was a really big thing for several reasons, the biggest one being my money situation. I was down to just a few dollars and I did not have three or four dollars to spend on a toothbrush and toothpaste, so if I had not burst into uncontrollable tears right then and there, I would have either had to spend money I couldn't afford on something that I shouldn't have had to spend money on, or I would have had to go without brushing my teeth for an unknown length of time. Yuck!

So here was another example for me that the universe really is friendly. I deliberately looked at it that way then, and I have never stopped being grateful to that man for treating me with respect and compassion as I stood there and cried in the lobby of his motel. It was a wonderful experience that I will never forget.

I took my brand new toothbrush and toothpaste upstairs to my room and I showered and brushed my teeth and then fell into that awesome bed. But instead of sleeping, I found that I was wide awake and worried about myself. I found myself focusing on the fact that I only had this wonderful place where I knew I was safe until 11:00 the next morning, and then what was I going to do? I wanted *(desperately needed!)* to go to sleep, and

I tried (frantically) to get myself to relax, but my mind emphatically refused to mellow out.

I finally realized that if I was ever going to be able to relax enough to fall asleep I was going to have to make some decisions first. As long as I felt like I was hanging there in thin air I was never going to be able to relax enough to fall asleep.

I dragged myself out of that bed and I found a phone book and I began making calls to every shelter and women's organization I could find. I was not looking for shelter. I know that shelters turn more people away than they are able to find beds for, so it's always been my feeling that those beds should be given to someone who has children to take care of, not an adult woman who is capable of taking care of herself. I was calling these places looking for suggestions. I wanted to know things like what part of town should I avoid? What services are available for a woman in my position? If it comes down to it and I need it, where might I find a mission that will give me a meal? Stuff like that.

Now this did not seem too difficult to me, but it sure turned out to be a problem for every single place I called! I had lived in Portland for most of my life and I would not have had any trouble telling someone who asked what part of town you're most likely to be raped or killed in if you're wandering around alone. I have only lived in the Phoenix metro area for a few years and I would not have any trouble answering that question here. But every one of the places I called said to me, "I'm sorry, we can't help you." The last place I called said, "I'm sorry, we can't help you, but let us know if you make it." Oh, my God! That one frustrated me so much that I didn't bother calling any more. I was done. These were domestic violence shelters that I was calling. They were supposed to care about women in my position, but the only thing any of them said to me was, "I'm sorry, we can't help you." I was amazed. I was discouraged. I was frustrated. I was very depressed. And I was terrified.

I used to speak of this in my capacity as a speaker for the Arizona Coalition Against Domestic Violence. In fact, this was usually what I talked about because my audiences were usually made up of domestic violence advocates who dealt with women in that position often. When they heard me tell my story it usually hit home with them how their attitude can impact someone else's life.

So I eventually found a positive way to use this particular experience, but at that time I was unbelievably frustrated. So, what to try next? I was having a pretty significant problem and I didn't know what to do next. There had to be a solution somewhere. But what?

> *I don't know what to do! Okay, what would I do if I DID know what to do? Oh, hey, I know what I can try…*

Mary Morrissey's church, the Living Enrichment Center (LEC), was huge, with a congregation of hundreds of people who actually drove to the church every Sunday. But there were also people who were interested in her teachings that didn't live close enough to make the drive, so they also had what were known as Living Enrichment Circles. These Circles existed all around the world and I knew that. And I knew that "all around the world" included the Phoenix metro area. So what if I called LEC and found out if there was a Circle anywhere near me? Just somebody I could connect with. Somebody who believed the things that I was learning to believe. I knew that if I could come in contact with somebody like that, whether they could help me or not, I would feel ever so much better just because I would not feel so alone.

I called the 800 number at LEC and a lady named Kathleen answered the phone. And guess what I did when she answered. Yep! I had a complete nervous breakdown right there in that poor woman's ear. I started to cry, and then I couldn't stop. She was wonderful! My thought at the time was that she was the most compassionate person on the planet. She just let me cry (and cry, and cry). She must have been able to tell that was what I needed to do just then, because she didn't try to get me to stop. She actually told me she'd stay on the phone with me for as long as I needed her to, and when I was ready she'd be there to listen. Of course, this made me cry even harder, partly out of shear relief to be in a place where I could just let go, but mainly because I wasn't used to that. I was used to being ridiculed and put down if I cried, so I always tried not to. I didn't quite know what to do in a situation where someone would just listen and not judge or tell me to "suck it up." But this lady was awesome. She told me to go ahead and let it out, and when she said that to me the floodgates opened and there was no stopping the river after that.

I don't know how long I just sat there and cried. It seemed like a really long time, but was probably less than five minutes. Remember the beginning of my journey, and the tears I cried on the bus as I was leaving Portland? Those tears left me feeling drained and hollow and depressed. Not these. These were healing tears. I was astonished at how much better I felt when I was able to stop. I can't say that I felt wonderful, but I was back to feeling like there might possibly be some hope for me.

When I was ready — and once again able to speak coherently — Kathleen was there to listen and to help in any way that she could. And she did, tremendously.

I explained what was happening with me, my whole situation up to and including what the shelters had all had to say to me. And then I asked her if there was a Living Enrichment Circle anywhere near me — somebody familiar with the Phoenix metro area who might be able to give me some suggestions. Somebody I could connect with. She did some checking and found that there was a Circle in Chandler (wherever *that* was). She took my number and said she was going to call the facilitator of that Circle, a lady named Kim, and that she would call me back shortly. And she did. She called me right back and told me that she had reached Kim and had explained my situation to her and asked her if she could give me a call. Kim immediately said that she would be happy to help. She took down my number and told Kathleen that she would call me right away. So Kathleen asked me to stay in touch with her and let her know periodically how I was doing. I promised that I would, and as we hung up I felt as if I might actually be okay. Maybe. Hopefully.

While I was waiting for Kim to call me I gave myself a little pep talk.

> *"The significant problems we face cannot be solved at the level of thinking that created those problems." Boy, I have found some problems, haven't I?! Well, it seems like calling LEC was a solution-level thought. Hopefully something will come of it. When is that Kim lady going to call? I hate this up-in-the-air feeling. I hate being by myself and not knowing what I'm going to do. Wait a minute! Knock off those kinds of thoughts! How much good is it going to do you to think thoughts like that? "Where I place my attention, I am placing my intention." Is it really your intention to go to the place that those miserable thoughts will take*

you? No, it's not, but it's so HARD to be positive right now! But do you really want to take the easy way out and fall back into the negativity that you're used to? It would be very easy to do that, but you KNOW what that road leads to, don't you? Yeah, more difficulties and a continuation of the hard, sad life that I have lived up until now. The whole idea behind leaving Portland was to start a new life, including a new way of thinking and looking at things! Did you think that was going to be easy? Well, guess what, I bet you could find a way to make it easier on yourself than what you're doing right now! If you tell yourself that it's HARD, you will create that for yourself. Remember what you did on the bus to turn things around when you were thinking these kinds of self-defeating thoughts and having these kinds of miserable, I-feel-so-sorry-for-myself feelings? What was it that you did? "Where I place my attention, I am placing my intention." What can you focus on that will not add to your feelings of "Just look at all my problems!" Oh yeah, how about looking for what you can be grateful for instead... Duh! Look around you right now and think about it! It's 11:00 in the morning and you have this room, this haven, this SAFE place for a whole 24 more hours. You do not have to worry that Jeff is going to show up and hurt you here because there is NO POSSIBLE WAY that he can know that you are here. (Unless, of course, you pick up your phone and call him, which you have no plans to do, right? Right!) Let's see, what else? Well, Kathleen and LEC are definitely worth feeling grateful for — there's no question about that. You got to this motel early enough to be able to benefit from the continental breakfast they had available, and since you brought some extra stuff up to your room, you will not go hungry today. And then breakfast will be avail-

able to you again tomorrow. This is a wonderful thing! Sooner or later, at some point during the 24 hours that this room is yours you WILL be able to lie down and sleep. And sleep. For as long as you need to. It's your choice how you handle what's happening in your life right now. You can allow yourself to freak out, and as a result of that you can be worried about yourself and the things that COULD happen to you, the things that MAY or MAY NOT happen to you. Or you can take advantage of what's happening IN THIS MOMENT – you can take it for what it is, which is a chance to relax, refresh, and regroup. This is a wonderful chance – a whole twenty-four hours – in which you can just let go and breathe and take things one moment at a time. Come on – it'll be good practice! But the phone's not ringing! Is that Kim person going to call? What will I do if she doesn't? I don't know... but why not give her at least thirty minutes before you decide that she's not going to call? Give her thirty minutes before you make this a reason to feel sorry for yourself.

It was right about the time that I was thinking that thought that my phone rang. I had previously decided that Kathleen was the most compassionate person on the planet. I had been wrong about that.

There is no such thing as coincidence and everything happens for a reason!

Could it be coincidence that the person that Kathleen got in touch with for me just happened to be a woman who was a victim advocate with the Chandler police department? A woman who just *happened* to share her compassionate self on a very regular basis with victims of domestic violence? Could it be coincidence that Kim was, without being a victim herself, just the person who could understand a little of what I was experiencing and be available to me from that place of compassion and wanting to help? I don't think so! It has been proven to me time and again over the years that there is no such thing as coincidence, and *this* was incredibly powerful proof of that.

There is no question in my mind that everything happens for a reason. If the shelters had been more helpful, my life would have turned out very differently than it has. If the shelters had been more helpful, I would not have found it necessary to call LEC. I never would have met Kim and her family, and the dominoes in my life would have fallen into very different places from where they actually landed.

When I answered my phone and found Kim on the other end of the line, I decided that I had been wrong about Kathleen being the most compassionate person on the planet. What I found in my conversation with Kim was that I had someone in the state of Arizona who cared about me, even though she had not met me and knew absolutely nothing about me. She was going to help me figure out what to do. She told me to try to relax and get some rest since I had the room I was in until the following day. And then the following morning she would come and pick me up and from there we would figure out what my options were.

Have you ever had your airway cut off and been unable to breathe? I have, more than once, and it's an awful feeling. And then when the pillow is lifted from your face or the hands are removed from around your throat, being able to take a breath is like being in heaven.

That was how I felt when my conversation with Kim ended. I had known that I was feeling pressure, but I don't think I had realized just how intense that feeling was until it lifted a little bit with that conversation.

When you're in a tunnel and you can't see the end of it, in fact you have no idea which way to turn to even *find* the end of it, the feeling of hopelessness is a lot like feeling as if you're suffocating. But then as you blunder around in the dark and you happen to come around a bend to where you can see just the barest glimmer of light, then not only do you regain your feeling of hope, but you also have something to move toward. It's still dark, and you know you still have some steps to take, but at least you can breathe and you have some light to focus on as you do take the steps that are necessary to bring you out of that tunnel.

As I hung up the phone I felt as if I had just blundered my way around the curve in my dark, dark tunnel and found my glimmer of light. That glimmer was a calm, soothing, compassionate voice on the phone, calling me "Honey" and assuring me that she would help me to be okay and that I no longer had reason to feel like I was all alone. Her name was Kim and I could not help but trust her.

Kim had told me to relax, take a breath, and get some rest, and now I finally felt able to do so. It was with an incredible sense of relief that I was able to close my eyes then and allow myself to go to sleep, instead of envisioning different scenarios of how I was going to die in Arizona... I was back to seeing the friendliness of the universe again, and with that I went to sleep, for about ten straight hours.

I woke up about 10:00 that night feeling like a different person—yet again. You know how you can practically see a baby grow while you're watching? They seem to change overnight sometimes, don't they? That was how I felt during this time – as if every time I turned around I had grown so much that I didn't recognize myself anymore.

I spent some time with myself that night, checking in with my feelings and trying to make sense of what I was thinking. This whole experience was a completely new thing for me. It was "undiscovered country" and I was finding myself somewhere between trusting my instincts and taking things as they came, and not trusting anything and being too terrified to take any steps at all. I kept going back and forth, back and forth. Worry—faith—worry—faith—worry—faith… It was like watching a ping pong ball. It took me a long time to realize I was doing that to myself again. But when I did realize it, and then realized that I *had* realized it, another piece seemed to fall into place for me in a big way. I could be my own worst enemy if I chose to. And it didn't have to be a conscious choice. In fact, it would never be a conscious choice. It would have to be a *conscious* choice to be my own friend. It would have to be a conscious choice to *notice* the thoughts that I was thinking and then control them instead of just letting them have free reign and go wherever they wanted to. I had thirty-five years of habitual thinking to change. And the first step to doing that *had* to be noticing where my thoughts were going in the first place.

I think it was the knowing it was safe to relax for a little while that helped me to be able to actually relax and notice what I was doing with my thoughts. Back and forth between, "I'm so scared, I don't know what I'm going to do!" and "I am safe right now, at least for a couple of days. Why not trust in a friendly universe and see what comes of that?"

I spent time that evening just taking things one moment at a time. I repeatedly found myself thinking, "Oh, my God, what am I going to do?!" kinds of thoughts. And whenever I noticed I was doing it, I just gently and lovingly pulled myself back to the knowledge that right in that moment I was safe and I had nothing to worry about. This being gentle and loving with myself was a very new thing for me. What I normally would have done to myself would have been to beat myself up and make myself feel bad.

> *Geez, you can't even hold onto a positive thought for five minutes! What's wrong with you? Everything's wrong with you — you don't ever do anything right! I don't know why you even bother to try! You know you're never going to get it right. You know it's not meant for you to be happy — that's why it's not possible for you to hang onto a positive thought! You might as well just give up now and put yourself out of your misery!*

It was an absolutely amazing feeling to be able to notice when I was doing that to myself and then to consciously pull myself out of that mindset in a loving and gentle way. Over and over again I would catch myself going to that place of judging myself on how bad I was at everything and who was I — really — to think I might be able to make a better life for myself? And every time I was able, sooner or later, to catch it at some point and turn it around for myself. *(I see you, Fear, and I know what you want. Thank you for trying to protect me, but you have no power over me.)*

Eventually I figured out that I could catch myself doing this to myself a lot sooner if I let go of trying to monitor my thoughts and paid attention to how I felt instead. There is a huge difference between feeling angry or disappointed with yourself and feeling gratitude and acceptance for yourself and your situation. As I paid more and more attention to how I was feeling emotionally, I noticed that as soon as I began feeling any kind of depression or frustration or hopelessness I just had to notice what I was thinking and I would see that I was thinking thoughts of depression, frustration, or hopelessness. And as soon as I could actually see what I was thinking, I could see that it was ME doing that thinking, and then I could CHANGE what I was thinking! How was I able to do it? By taking my attention *off* what was making me feel bad and putting it *on* what I had to be grateful for.

    This is an amazing technique that can be used to change how you feel in any given moment. The most difficult thing about it is remembering to do it when you're in the middle of taking yourself down the spiral of feeling powerless, depressed or hopeless. Catch yourself thinking the thoughts that are causing the feelings and then—gently and lovingly (in other words, without beating yourself up for being where you are in your thoughts)—find some different thoughts. Think of anything you can that you can appreciate, and as you notice one thing and express feelings of gratitude for that one thing, it will be that much easier to notice the next thing and the next thing that you can feel grateful for!

    This takes practice, and you have to really concentrate on it at first. And this particular night I did it deliberately and consciously and with lots of appreciation for the things I had learned during my trip to Phoenix. I continuously reminded myself that I could look at things however I chose to look at them. And however I chose to look at what was happening would determine my experience of whatever was happening. (Yes, this was easy to tell myself — not so easy to do. In fact, years later, this is still something that I have to consciously remind myself of. It is, and I'm it sure will always remain, something that I have to *practice*.)

Eventually I made it back to sleep, and when I woke up early the next morning I was still afraid, wondering what was going to happen to me, but I was also excited, wondering what was going to happen to me! There was no more comfort zone for me — I was now in uncharted territory. This is an amazing (terrifying, exciting, uncomfortable) feeling, let me tell you!

> *My history need not determine my destiny. My history does not HAVE to determine my destiny! I will not LET my history determine my destiny, dammit! I do not want to keep experiencing the life that I have lived up until now. I want a new experience of my life. I want to be involved with people who are compassionate and do not feel a need to make other people feel bad. I want to know people who believe the things that I am learning to believe. I want to create my own life, instead of letting other people tell me what I should do and how I should live. I want to decide for myself what makes me happy. I want to decide for myself what I want to experience. I want to learn to use my faith in myself to create the life I want to be living. I want to learn to trust my own decision-making abilities. I want to make my own decisions, take responsibility for the results I get, and see what my life looks like. And then I'll make my next (own) decision based on those results. And as I continue to do this, I will create a new life for myself — I will create the life that I WANT to be living!*

Kim called me that morning to let me know that her husband, Alan, would be there to pick me up at about 10:00 a.m. As I waited for him to show up I practiced not being a complete basket case. I was nervous, scared, and uncomfortable and I knew it wouldn't take much to send me over the edge if I wasn't careful. I decided that going over the edge would be taking the easy way out. I would be letting myself off the hook if I allowed myself to give up. I really wanted to see how strong I could be if I just made the effort.

As Alan put my duffel bag in the back of their Forerunner and I climbed in the front, I felt myself taking another "step in Faith" as I put my trip from Portland behind me and turned to face whatever I would find in front of me.

Chapter 9

One Step (in Faith) at a Time

"We are what we think. All that we are arises with our thoughts. With our thoughts we make our world."
~ The Buddha

The further Alan drove toward their home in Chandler, the smaller I felt. I was amazed — and very distressed — as I saw just how huge the Phoenix metro area was. What had I gotten myself into? What was I going to do? I didn't have a car. I didn't have a job. I had less than $20 left. Was I insane to think I was going to be able to make it here? Why did I pick such a big, hot, bright, intimidating place to run to? Everything was the same color — how was I ever going to learn where anything was if it all looked the same?

I have no idea what Alan thought of me during that drive. I'm sure we had some sort of conversation, but if we did, there was only a small part of me engaged in it. The other parts of me were at war in my head. The terror-stricken part of me showed up in full force pretty much as soon as we got on our way away from the motel. I felt as if I was suffocating in my fear as we drove along. It had a death grip on me and I knew that if I couldn't break free from it I was going to have another breakdown. I'd had enough of breakdowns with the one the previous day, thank you very much. I needed to get my own grip back. I knew that I needed to be bigger than my fear — I needed to get it back under control or I was going to lose myself to it again.

So I deliberately thought of all the stuff I had learned over the last few days. Mainly that "A new thought creates a new thing." If I continued along these lines of depression and fear, what was I going to get? What would doing what I had always done — letting my fear have control of my decisions — accomplish for me? I would find myself right back in the same kind of situation I had always created for myself. I would either end up latching onto the first guy I came across in hopes that he would take care of me (yeah, *that* had always worked well for me in the past, hadn't it?), or I would give up and call Jeff. I would stick my tail between my legs and go home and take my punishment for the rest of what would be left of my life if I let my fear make my decisions for me.

Where would a "new" thought take me? What if I looked to the solution level of my situation instead of focusing on the problem? What if I made my decisions based on faith that things could work out well for me, instead of letting my fear be in control? What if I allowed myself to relax and just took each thing as it came, instead of looking at it all as one huge mountain of "this is my problem — oh my God, what am I going to do?" Had I given up on my friendly universe already? No, I had not!

> *So what is my situation, really? I am a young, healthy, intelligent woman who happens to be starting over. I am not the first woman in the world to ever do*

this, and if others have successfully done it, why can't I? I can look back at my history and see all the times that I have sabotaged myself and prevented myself from having a good life, just out of my habit of believing that I wasn't worthy of having a good life. But am I not in the process, right now, of learning that my history does not have to determine my destiny? Am I not, right now, in the process of teaching myself that just because that's what my life has always been like does not mean that I have to continue to have those same kinds of experiences now? Look at what I have accomplished so far! Now is not the time to give up or give in! That is how I've always handled things. I've always given up because I was making my decisions from a place of not believing that I deserved to have a better life. Well, you know what? I do deserve to have a good life! I deserve to be happy! I deserve to like myself! I deserve to be strong and trust myself to make good decisions! I deserve to feel safe in my own life! The first thing I ever heard Mary Morrissey say was that we all deserve to have our Dreams come true. I did not believe her then. Do I believe that now? I have been telling myself that I do. Am I telling myself the truth? Do I believe that I deserve to live the life of my Dreams? Or how about if I put it this way: Do I WANT to believe that I deserve to live my Dreams? Or do I WANT to believe that I am a piece of crap who doesn't deserve to live a good life? Isn't that what it boils down to? Do I want to believe something that makes me feel good and excited and worthy? Or do I want to believe something that makes me feel bad, small, and defeated? Is my universe friendly? Or hostile? Haven't I learned lately that the answer to that question is completely up to me and how I choose to look at it? How about if I just

> *get right down to it and ask myself this: Do I want to be happy? Or do I want to be unhappy? The answer to that question, also, is completely up to me, isn't it? Can I be this scared and still find things to be grateful for? Why not try it and see?*

As I sat in the passenger seat and looked out at all that brown bigness, I asked myself what I had to be grateful for right then and there. I looked at my fear for what it was and I basically thanked it for sharing and told it to take the back seat for now. What did I have, right now — *in this moment* — to be grateful for? I was in an air-conditioned vehicle with a man who, out of the kindness of his heart, had driven twenty miles to come and pick me up and get me out of a messed up situation. He and his wife knew nothing about me — *at all*. Yet they were in the process of doing what they could to help me get on my feet. Alan was nice. He was not pushing me to answer questions and I could feel no judgment coming from him at all. That alone would have been enough. But there was also this fact that sort of hit me all of a sudden. These were people who knew about Mary Manin Morrissey and the principles that she taught! The last few days I had been immersed in her teachings, but I had been doing it all by myself. I was on my way to spend time with a family who believed the same stuff I had been learning to believe for myself! They would be able to help me stay on track! I would have a support system, hopefully. I would have somebody to call if I got frustrated and felt like giving up! This realization brought me the rest of the way up and out of the "problem." I still hadn't met Kim, but I had spoken to her on the phone, and her husband was a nice man. I was encouraged. And I was getting better and better at pulling myself out of feeling "down" whenever I headed in that direction. I realized that I still had far more to be grateful for than I did to complain about, and this was a wonderful thing! The fear was still there, but it was firmly buckled into the back seat and it seemed to be staying there for the time being. My universe was back to being friendly and I could feel myself breaking lifelong habits of thought as we pulled up to Kim and Alan's home in Chandler.

Alan was a very nice, friendly man. My impression of Kim when I met her was that she could only be an angel. I wouldn't have been surprised if I had seen wings sprout from her shoulder blades. She was tall and gorgeous. She was soft-spoken and gentle, and compassion seemed to radiate from her whole being. She is still my friend and I still see all of these things in her. She is one of the most beautiful people—inside and out—that I have ever met and I have never stopped being grateful that I know her.

As we sat in her living room and talked I realized, again, that how I experienced my life was completely up to me. When I left Portland, it was with the attitude that I was going to make it, and I was going to do it all by myself. As I sat there in Kim's living room I thought about how unrealistic that attitude had been. No matter how big of a chip I created on my shoulder, that chip was not going to contribute anything to my success in making a good life for myself. If anything, that kind of attitude—that chip—would *get in the way* of what I wanted for myself. I also thought about the fact that if I really believed that the universe was friendly and on my side, I would believe that It wanted me to make it and that help would show up when I needed it. As I sat there with Kim

I realized that it had to be okay to accept help along my path because that was a *part* of my path!

When I had left Portland, it was with the idea that I was going to prove that I could make it on my own—without help from anybody. Come hell or high water, I was going to do it all by myself and as I did so, that would be my proof that I was "worthy" of having a good life. The biggest problem with that was that I was *expecting* "hell or high water," which meant that I was expecting it to be difficult. I was *expecting* to have to struggle, to have to overcome incredibly huge obstacles, to have to "make it through."

As I sat there with Kim, she told me that she and Alan had reserved a room for me at a motel that was only about a mile from their house. She was following her intuition, and getting me a room was what felt like the right thing for them to do. The chip on my shoulder immediately objected to my accepting help of any kind, and I had a rough time getting it to shut up so I could hear the intelligent, rational part of myself. *That* part of me said:

> *You will not make it if you try to do it all by yourself and you know it. Accepting help from these people does not mean that Jeff was ever right when he called you a mooch. Think about it. When he called you that, who was the one who was working two jobs so you wouldn't lose your house? It was you, not him. What was he doing at that time? He was lying on the couch, watching TV all day and getting angry because you weren't there to clean house or cook dinner. Who was REALLY the mooch? It was not you! You have let that bother you for far too long – don't you think that now is a good time to let go of it? As long as you carry that around with you,*

> *it's going to keep getting in the way. You can accept help from these people without becoming — or feeling like — a mooch! You can accept help from these people and just be grateful for their help. It's okay to do that. You are a good person and you deserve to be happy. Relax and accept this help as a part of your journey into your better life. Just try it and see what happens. Accept it as an opportunity to begin your healing.*

Accepting that kind of help, which was not what I had been looking for, was a difficult thing for me to do. That part of me that felt as if it needed to prove something to the world (or at least to all the people in my life who had ever told me I was worthless) had a really hard time letting go of that need. I repeatedly had to remind myself to set it down. As long as I kept picking up that need to prove something and carrying it around, my hands would be too full to accept the gift that was being offered to me.

Kim and I sat and talked for a while, and I explained my situation to her. She asked me what she could do to help and we made plans for the next day. And then she drove me over to the motel.

It was a nice motel in Chandler that was about a mile from Kim and Alan's house. She said she wanted me close, "just in case." I got the feeling that she was afraid I was entertaining thoughts of suicide. This was a very uncomfortable feeling, to think that somebody might think that I would consider taking my own life. I will admit that in my past I have experienced thoughts and feelings of, "Why bother?" I had also occasionally wondered who would actually give a rip if I were to die. But I had never actively considered killing myself, mainly because I have always been far too curious about what my future has in store for me. And in the times that I didn't care about that I had always placed my focus on what my children's futures hold for them (and for me). I think the biggest reason I never actively considered committing suicide is that my mom did try it—several times. I always wondered how she could so easily give up and leave me. I was not the best or most stable of mothers, but it was the thought of how my kids would feel if I were to kill myself that was the biggest reason that I never seriously considered it.

When Kim said, "...just in case." my first thought was to assure her that I would never do that. Then I decided that I was jumping to the conclusion that she was thinking that about me, so I did my best let it go.

She helped me take my things upstairs to my room, so she'd know where I was. We talked for a few more minutes and she said to me, "Call me if you need me. I don't care what time it is—day or night. You call me if you need me! Right now you are exhausted. I can see it in your face. I want you to rest and relax and not worry about anything. We're going to help you through this! You're not alone!"

This, of course, caused me to burst into tears. They were tears of gratitude and relief, but they also served to let me know just how exhausted I really was.

Kim left me to myself then, with another admonishment to call her if I needed anything—anything at all—and a reminder of all the stuff we were going to accomplish the next day.

As I look back on that Thursday, I can remember how overwhelmed I felt. Sitting here, reliving what I was feeling then, I realize that I was not just exhausted and afraid and excited. I was in shock. During the previous week I had put myself through some *very* traumatic experiences. I felt like I was losing it big time. I am so thankful that I did not give in to those feelings!

After Kim left I came to an abrupt realization that I could continue to be afraid if I chose to, but I didn't really *need* to. At this point in time there was really no way that Jeff would be able to find me. Up until the previous morning when I had left the bus station it had been in my best interest to keep my fear of him finding me alive. However, when I left the bus station, just about any chance of him finding me ceased to exist. I had paid for the previous night's room with cash, so it would have taken a miracle for him to find me there. And now the room I was in was in Kim's name, so there was no chance at all of him finding me here. Imagine my feelings of absolute relief when I realized this! I *could* rest, and I *could* relax. I could safely let go of some of the anxiety that I had been hanging onto as a means of self-protection and self-preservation. I could let my guard down a little bit! When I came to that conclusion I was absolutely convinced that relief was the best feeling I had ever experienced!

I consciously and deliberately talked myself into relaxing and getting comfortable. It was wonderful!

The first thing I did was to pick up my phone and call both of my kids to let them know I was okay. I had called Melissa from the bus in Portland and let her know that I was leaving and that I'd call her when I had some sort of idea what I was going to do. So I called her first and let her know that I was all right and that I had met some people who were going to help me get a grip on my situation. My poor daughter had been really worried about me and it was great to be able to call her and tell her positive things about what was going on.

Next I called my son, Kyle. This was a little more difficult because he had no idea that I had left Portland. And I had left without saying good-bye. The best thing about this conversation was that I got to point out to him that I could call and talk to him any time I wanted to now. Jeff had not allowed me to talk to my kids, so whenever I did it was always uncomfortable in one way or another, either because he would be standing there listening to everything I said—ready to find something to get angry about. Or I would be doing it behind his back, knowing that if (when) he found out, it would be just one more thing he could use against me to prove how untrustworthy I was. So now I was not with Jeff any more. He would not be monitoring my phone minutes to see what I was doing wrong. He could not stop me from calling my children whenever I wanted to. He could not stop me from getting to know them again! I was ecstatic and excited about this! I didn't really know my kids at all any more and I was indescribably happy that I would be able to be a part of their lives again, even if it was long distance over the phone. At least it was *something*, instead of no contact at all! So Kyle was as happy about this as I was, and he understood when I told him that I didn't let him know I was leaving because that would have just given him cause to worry about me. And he completely agreed that he would have done that.

So now, from Kyle and Melissa's point of view, they just had to wait and see if I could make it in Arizona. Actually, they were waiting to see how long it would be before I gave up and went back. They were hopeful, while at the same time trying not to get their hopes up, that I'd be able to do it this time. They both figured that if they didn't get their hopes up, they wouldn't be too disappointed if I wasn't able to do it.

I find it pretty sad that parents say to their children, and people say to each other, "Don't get your hopes up, because it might not work out." I have come to believe that it would be so much more helpful if people would instead say, "Keep your hopes up, because it could very well work out!" This would serve to make people far more likely to look for ways to get things to work out the way they want them to, don't you think? They would be more likely to think along the lines of, "What can I do to make this work for me?" Or, "What's a solution here?" Or, "What's a different choice I can make here, that will have a positive outcome?"

If you ever want to set someone up to fail, just tell them, "Don't get your hopes up." And then watch what they do. Most people will give up before they really even get started! Think about it. I used to tell myself that all the time. I learned it from my mother—she used to tell herself (and me) the same thing. We each used to say, "I'm not going to get my hopes up, that way I won't be too disappointed when it doesn't work out." And when things didn't go the way we wanted them to we would always say, "I knew it wasn't going to work out. I sure am glad I didn't get my hopes up!" Sad. What I think is even more sad is that those who do this are just trying to protect the people they love from getting hurt! I know that was always my intention whenever I said it to my kids, and that was always my mother's intention when she said it to me. It was never out of a desire to be unsupportive or cruel. It was always with the best of intentions. It kind of makes me sick now, to think of all the times I have cautioned my kids not to get their hopes up for anything instead of supporting their hopes and doing my level best to help them experience the things they were hoping for. Now that I understand this, I think that, "Don't get your hopes up." is one of the most disempowering things I have ever said, either to myself or to another person.

I am so thankful that I have learned that there really can be (in fact, is) joy in the journey! That makes it so much easier to encourage people to go for their dreams.

So from the kids' point of view, they were still in the mode of, "I'll believe it when I see it. You've left him so many times before, and you've always gone back. Why should we think you won't go back again?" And I completely understood where they were coming from because that thought had crossed my mind more than once during those first few days. They would believe it when they saw it.

Then there was *my* point of view. From my point of view, it would be worth it to me to stick it out and make it on my own just for the reward of being able to love and communicate with my children! It would be completely and utterly worth it to me to keep my hopes up — to stay focused on what I wanted to create for myself instead of what I was afraid *might* happen to me! It would be worth it to me to work toward that, keeping my attention on all the things I wanted to experience. If I could do that with a positive attitude, believing it was possible, then I would get the things I wanted!

It is so strange to look back on this now, knowing how it has turned out. At that time I was doing it all on faith. I had never done anything on faith before in my life, and here I was practicing "just knowing" that things would work out if I stayed focused on what I wanted and kept my attention there. Always before — throughout my entire life — I had held the belief that I could never have the life I really wanted to experience. I had only believed in the littleness and pain that *was* my life experience.

Now here I was in this motel room in the process of creating a whole new personal belief system for myself. Have you ever heard the term, "Quantum leap?" That was what I accomplished for myself during those first few days after I left Portland. I had spent the previous nine months practicing and preparing myself, reading *Building Your Field of Dreams* over and over again, and making that little shift in direction that was meant to take me to "a whole new place." Now here I was in my "whole new place" and I could do with it whatever I chose to do. I am so grateful to Mary Morrissey for the work that she has done that gets these wonderful principles out there for people like me to grab onto and apply to our lives! I would never have been able to get myself safely through those first few days without her. No, I would have fallen right back into my own personal downward spiral countless times during those first few days if I had been doing it with my previous belief system. And I would be dead now—there is no question about that.

After re-establishing contact with my kids, I called my friend Violet. We had worked together for the previous seven years and she was (and still is) one of my best friends.

I called her at work to let her know I was okay and to find out what Jeff was up to. She was very relieved and happy to hear from me, not only because she wanted to know that I was okay, but also because Jeff was flipping out. (Whew! That meant he was still in Portland! Yay!! In my mind I was doing handsprings!)

"What's he doing?"

"Oh God! He is pissed! He's not sleeping and he's not working."

I was so thankful to be able to ask the burning question, "He doesn't have any idea where I am, does he?"

"No! He thinks you went to Texas with Janet!"

Janet had been the manager of the store where Violet and I worked. She had never been intimidated by Jeff. In fact, *he* was the one who was intimidated by *her* because she wasn't afraid to stand up to him. Three days before I left, Janet and her husband had moved to Texas because Janet had received a huge promotion. Jeff knew this, and so, since Janet had helped me in my situation with him before, he just naturally assumed that I had gone with them. This made a lot of sense, because it would have been perfect.

I had never felt freer in my life than I did right then, when Violet told me where he thought I had gone. I knew in that moment that I no longer had to worry about him finding me because he would never consider confronting Janet. He knew that Janet wouldn't put up with *any* of the things he was capable of pulling.

So instead of jumping in his truck and coming after me, and instead of hiring a private investigator to look for me (which he had threatened me with before), he quit working and he fell into depression. Because he quit going to work, he lost his job. As a result of that he lost both the trailer we had been living in and his truck. Basically he lost everything he had, and he blamed all of that on me. If I hadn't left, he would have continued to go to work. And if he had continued to go to work he wouldn't have lost everything.

On the other hand, if I had stayed he would have killed me and then he'd have ended up back in prison. But that would have been my fault, too. Ah well, what can I do? It has become my sincere wish for him that he — somehow, some way — discovers that he is responsible for his own happiness. Until he figures that out, he will never be happy. And when he *does* finally figure that out for himself, he will never feel the need to hurt another person again. It brings me incredible joy to look forward to that for him.

For myself though, I am very thankful that he decided I went to Texas. I cannot even begin to describe the relief that I felt when Violet told me that. I was free! I was free to focus on creating the life I wanted to live!

Chapter 10

Freedom, Fear, and Letting Go

"...in this moment, we have the opportunity to wash the slate clean and begin again."
~ Mary Manin Morrissey

The discovery that Jeff was convinced that I went to Texas released an incredible amount of tension in both my body and my emotions. That feeling of relief was palpable. I actually felt the muscles in my jaw, around my eyes and forehead, and in my shoulders let go of the tension that I had grown so accustomed to over the previous several days. The knowledge that he wasn't going to step into my field of vision at any moment and punch me in the head was such a huge load off my mind that I felt as if I should be floating up next to the ceiling!

That feeling lasted for about two minutes, and then my desperate need to be loved by somebody — anybody — showed its sad, wounded face to me.

So THIS is what it feels like to be free! Amazing! He's not coming after you — he's not even going to try to find you! You are free to make a new life for yourself! You don't have to worry that he's going to show up and punch you in the head, pull out your hair, run you over with his truck, or drag you back to Portland — this is wonderful!

Wait! He's not even going to try? But what about all that, "I love you I need you I can't live without you" stuff he used to say? What about all that, "It's you and me forever, baby" stuff? I know, I know, it always sounded like a threat when he said it, but at least there was some element of feeling wanted in there. Now what do I have? He's not even going to bother to try! He never loved me like he said he did. He just wanted me so he'd have someone to dominate. Isn't this proof enough that I'll never be loved by anybody? How long am I going to keep this up? Why should I even bother to try? I'm all alone and nobody is ever going to love me the way I want to be loved. I hate my life.

Now wait just a minute! Are you paying attention to what you're doing to yourself? You are doing the opposite of what you decided on the bus. Didn't you decide that you were not going to worry about how others felt about you? Didn't you decide that you were going to practice loving yourself and being responsible for your own happiness, instead of depending on somebody else to make you happy? Did you not decide that you were going to look for things to be grateful for in whatever circumstance you found yourself in? So what's all this, "Nobody's ever gonna love me" crap? You know that the more you think thoughts like that the worse you're going to feel. How long are **you** going to do this to **yourself**? And, by the way, you do realize that it is you doing this to yourself, don't you? He's not doing anything to make you feel this way and you know it! He only has the power to make you feel bad if you give it to him. And he's not responsible for your feelings, choices, or actions any more than you are responsible for his.

But what about him blaming me for the problems he's having? I need to call him and set him straight! I need to get him to admit that none of his troubles are my fault! I need to get him to admit to HIS responsibility in all this! I can't let him get away with placing all the blame on me! I know he's telling everyone that I screwed him over, just like he's done before. He's probably telling everyone that I took off with all his money and ran away with some guy. I don't want people to believe that about me! I don't want people believing I'm the piece of shit he says I am! I have to stop him! I have to convince him that he's the one who pushed me away! I have to make him admit that this is all HIS fault!!!

Hey! You're doing it again. Look at the train of thought you just climbed on. It's time to switch tracks now. You know that anybody who matters to you is not going to believe anything that spews out of his mouth, right? And how much does it really matter if people you don't even know or care about believe the stuff that he says? This is not something you need to worry about or focus on right now! Where you place your attention is where you're placing your intention. Keep that in mind! Do you really want to keep your attention on blaming him for all of your problems? You realize that if you do that, you're doing the same thing that you're accusing him of doing to you. Can you see that? Knock it off! Focus on what you want, not what you don't want! If you focus on what you hate or what you don't want, it will CONSUME you! Let it go! Stop looking at the stuff that's behind you. Stop looking at the stuff that you can't do anything about! I know it's not easy, but you are making this a lot harder on yourself than it really needs to be. Let go of needing to prove to others that you are good. Concentrate on knowing that for yourself and the rest will follow. Focus on being the person that you want to be, and others will see you that way. But as long as you spend your time trying to make him admit his "wrongness" you won't have the time or the energy you'll need to make this new life work for you. Decide what you want. Do you want to be right? Or do you want to be happy? In this situation you cannot have both. Let it go. Focus on what you want. Don't worry about the stuff that you can't do anything about. Breathe. Relax. Focus on what you want. What is it that you want? You want to be happy. How can you be happy if you're looking at all this stuff that makes you feel bad? Focus on the truth about you. You are strong. You are intelligent. You are a good person and you deserve to be happy and have your dreams come true! Focus on that, and let go of the stuff that doesn't matter. That stuff has no power unless you give it power. Take the wind out of its sails and let go of it. Your attention to it is giving it the wind that it needs to keep its sails filled. Your attention to it is what's keeping it active in your mind. Let it go. Set it down. It is not attached to you, and you can let go of it any time you choose. How long do you really want to do this to yourself? Practice being the person you want to be and don't worry about what he's doing or saying. You are in control of you. Let go of your need to make him wrong. That need does not serve you and you know it.

You cannot face the future if you're placing all your attention on what's past. Face forward and look at what's in front of you! Face forward and take the steps that you need to take to get you to where you want to go, and you will end up where you want to be!

As I talked myself up out of the despair that I had been heading for, I realized that what I had been doing to myself just then was something that I really was doing to myself, all by myself. I could not blame that on Jeff, nor could I blame it on my circumstances. He was fifteen hundred miles away, wallowing in his own self-pity, and my circumstances had no control over my thoughts. Circumstances are just circumstances — that's all they *can* be. My circumstances had no power to make me miserable or upset unless I gave them that power. What I came to realize just then — more deeply than ever before — was that how I chose to deal with my circumstances would determine what kind of life I would create for myself in Arizona.

I hated knowing that Jeff was blaming me for the problems he was having, but I decided that I could look at this as an opportunity to practice knowing that I was not responsible for any of the choices that he happened to make for himself. I decided to leave it at that because I knew myself well enough to know that if I chose to dwell on it I would fall right back into the need to prove to him that his situation was not my fault and I would sabotage any chance for success that presented itself to me. So, he was responsible for his own choices and his own actions. And I was now free to be responsible for mine!

Before Kim left me alone in my room, she had admonished me to do my best to relax and get some rest. I found that, as a result of talking to my kids and Violet (and then myself), I was able to let go and just be. And that's what I did for the rest of that day. I tried not to think about anything that worried or scared me, and I was somewhat successful. It's hard to break a life-long habit of worry and fear, but I knew if I was going to successfully create a good life for myself in Arizona, that was a necessary thing for me to do. And I needed to start right now! So I spent the rest of that day with

Mary Morrissey and *Building Your Field of Dreams*, feeling encouraged by all the positive things I was in the middle of learning from her. And feeling very grateful that I was finally in a place in my life in which I could change the things in myself that I needed to change in order for me to live my life happy.

The following day, Friday, Kim picked me up in the morning and we began our running around with the intention of getting my feet underneath me.

The first thing we did was drive out to Scottsdale Fashion Square Mall. Why? One of the things that Violet had told me during our phone conversation the previous day was that she had over-nighted my check to a store in that mall that was owned by the same company that owned the store in Portland. All I needed to do was get there and I would have some money to start with. What a relief to have my check in my hand!

From there we went and opened a checking account for me, and then we headed for the temporary agency where I would apply to work for Motorola. Alan worked for Motorola, so he knew they were looking for people. But you had to go through the temp agency to get hired on, and then you had to pass a series of tests called the BATB tests. So this day Kim took me to Kelly Services and we got the ball rolling. I put in my application and made an appointment for the following Monday for an interview and to do the aptitude tests.

And then she took me back to my motel room, where I spent the rest of that day and the following day just trying to relax and feel what it felt like to be on my own and strong.

Kim and Alan had paid for me to stay in that room for two nights—Thursday and Friday. On Friday Kim told me that her parents were feeling called to help, too, so they paid for another night. And then on Saturday Kim's sister decided that it was right for her to help, too.

By Saturday, though, I was feeling uncomfortable about other people paying for one night at a time when I had money of my own. Kim assured me that it was okay and that no one minded. In fact, they all thought I should hang onto the money I had for as long as I could. But that just did not feel right to me. It was all right for me to accept their help when I had nothing, but I needed to know that I could do it on my own. That was a huge thing for me, and it was something that I wanted to know for myself. I knew in my heart that nobody really thought I could do it, but I also knew in my heart that I was in the process of growing and changing. I was becoming the person that I had always wanted to be, but that I had never before had the courage to allow myself to become.

I was practicing following my Guidance, my still small Voice that Mary talks about so often. That Guidance, that Voice, let me know that it was time to step out of the limbo that I had been in for the previous two days. That limbo had been a wonderful place to be. It had been a place to relax and begin to heal. But I couldn't stay there forever. If I wanted to move forward, I had to move forward.

On Saturday Kim said to me, "I've told my sister about you and your situation and she's feeling called to help, too. She wants to pay for another night for you to stay here."

I said, "I've been thinking. I am uncomfortable staying here and letting your family pay for this room on a night to night basis. I'll be grateful to accept help from your sister, but what if we put her contribution toward one of those motel rooms that you can get by the week? I would feel so much better about that. I know that your family is not rich and that you can't afford to keep renting this room for me indefinitely. I got my check yesterday, so I have a little bit of money. I would feel so much better if I knew I had a place to stay for a whole week. And it would also feel wonderful to know that I'm taking some responsibility for myself and my situation."

Kim did not agree with me. She said, "I don't think that's a good idea. You've been through so much! I think you should just let us take care of you for a while, until you get on your feet."

In *Building Your Field of Dreams* Mary Morrissey tells a story about her daughter at the age of four in a public swimming pool in Portland. The whole family used to go there regularly in the summertime. They would all swim and laugh and play and have a great time. Except for Mary's daughter, who clung to the edge of the pool for dear life. She could see with her own eyes that everybody was having a wonderful time and that nobody was getting hurt. But this little four-year-old could not get past her fear, even though she could see other kids that were her age and size out there in the middle of the pool having the time of their lives. Mary and her husband did everything they could think of to convince this little girl that she would be okay of she would let go, but nothing worked. Until one day she finally decided that she was ready. She was done being on the fringes of the fun, and she was done trying to enjoy herself with only one hand, while desperately clinging to the edge of the pool with the other. This day she decided to let go and trust that she would be okay. So she did, and she was, and with that one action she changed her whole experience of being in that pool.

Kim knew this story just as well as I did, so she understood what I meant when I said I felt it was time for me to let go of the edge of the pool and trust that I would be okay. I said, "Don't get me wrong. It would be really easy for me to just keep clinging to the edge, to keep accepting your family's help day after day. And I would continue to be grateful for all of your help. But I really, honestly feel that it would be much healthier for me to let go and start doing some of this on my own. I know that this is the right thing for me to do, and I have complete faith that I'll be fine. I'm trusting my Intuition on this. It just feels like this is what I'm supposed to do."

Kim could see that I was serious, that I meant what I was saying. She understood exactly what I was talking about, but she had a really hard time accepting that this was what would be best for me. She wanted to take care of me, and she didn't want me to have to worry about anything. She wanted to rescue me. And I had to tell her that she already had. When a firefighter pulls someone out of a burning building, he doesn't carry them around on his shoulders for the rest of their life, right? No. He sets them down with a feeling of satisfaction and fulfillment, and they go on to live their life in gratitude for that firefighter who rescued them in their time of needing to be rescued. I could not have survived those three days as successfully as I had if I'd had to do it on my own. That was a fact. But now it was time for me to be set onto my own two feet to walk on my own to the middle of the pool and trust that I wouldn't drown.

It took some effort, but I finally convinced Kim that this was the right thing for me to do. I could tell she wasn't happy with my decision, but she could clearly see my point. I needed to let go and trust. And so did she.

I spent some time that evening making phone calls and continuing to trust my feelings. I called one place in Phoenix that was advertising rooms for $75 per week. The guy that answered sounded like an extremely angry person. He said, "The desert is a mean place to live and if you're smart you'll leave now." I thanked him and decided that I didn't care how cheap the room was, I did not want to be around somebody with an attitude like that. Ick!

I made call after call, until finally I found a place in Tempe on Apache Blvd. The weekly rent was $165 and they did have a vacancy. I decided I could swing that for at least one week. And then I just allowed myself to trust that I'd figure out what to do next when the time came to decide what to do next.

What a feeling! As I sat in my room in Chandler the following morning thinking about it, I came to some abrupt and profound realizations. I had come a long way in just six days. Less than a week before this I had been frantically trying to keep my eyes on every entrance into the bus station in Portland. I had lived through the fear of Jeff finding me before I left. I had lived through the fear, anger, and discomfort of a two-day bus ride in which I left everything I knew and loved behind, and came to a place in which I had nothing that I knew or loved. I had lived through the fear of him possibly being at the bus station in Phoenix when I arrived, ready to beat the hell out of me and take me back to Portland. I had lived through spending my first night in Phoenix alone in the bus station. I had trusted my instincts when they told me not to take the easy way out with Michelle/April, and I had again trusted them when they told me that it was right to spend most of the money I had left on one night in a motel. When calling the shelters did not work out for me, I had followed the guidance I had felt to call the Living Enrichment Center. And then I had been able to set my pride aside and accept help from Kim and Alan, rather than killing myself trying to do it all alone. I had been able to talk myself up from despair to hopefulness and optimism in a matter of minutes, so now I knew it could be done. I was learning how to let go of things that bothered me, and place my attention on things that made me happy. I was learning that by letting go of those things that bothered me, I was making it possible for myself to tap in to the happiness that was there inside me at all times, just waiting for me to notice it! And I was learning that I could do the things that felt right for me to do, even when I was scared out of my mind.

I had not even been away from Portland for a week yet, and already I felt like a brand new person. I had grown so much, and come so far, that I could never be the same again.

Now I just needed to find out who the real me was. I needed to continue trusting myself and see where that would lead me. And I was free to do just that. What an adventure!

Chapter 11

Loneliness, Successes, and Non-Prostitution

*"Our grand business is not to see
what lies dimly at a distance,
but to do what lies clearly at hand."
~ Thomas Carlyle*

Sunday morning, July 2, 2000 Kim picked me up and gave me a ride to the motel in Tempe. She was still unhappy about my decision to move. I discovered later that when she saw the place that I was moving to she became even more worried. Well, you get what you pay for, you know? And for $165 per week, I got an absolute dump that was not in a very good part of town. I found out for myself the first time I stepped out the door just what that part of town was like. During my entire stay in that room I repeatedly had to deal with guys who wanted to either buy me or sell me. Talk about an adventure!

After Kim reluctantly left me on my own I went for a walk to try to familiarize myself with the neighborhood and to find the nearest grocery store. I just wanted to get my bearings. It was then that I learned that I had landed myself in what is known as "Hooker Alley." Oh, joy! I repeatedly had to inform people that I wasn't a prostitute. I decided that, rather than being offended by all this, I could handle it with a sense of humor and just let it be what it was. It was people jumping to conclusions because of what they could see, instead of looking deeper to find out the truth of my situation. It's my opinion that dealing with those people with a sense of humor instead of getting upset is what saved me from getting hurt. After all, I was in a potentially dangerous position. I could have been forced at any time and there wouldn't have been much that I could have done about it. I think that my being good natured about it and treating it as humorous helped them to see it as humorous and almost every one of those guys took the news with some chagrin at having jumped to that particular conclusion. I usually ended up getting some kind of back-handed compliment such as, "Oh—too bad!" or "Oh, bummer!" Too funny! It's still funny, and it's fun to remember, because I know that if I hadn't changed my way of looking at things, that particular experience would have been *very* different from what it was.

That whole experience taught me a lot about both judging other people by appearances and having compassion for people who find themselves in that kind of situation.

I spent Monday morning calling temporary agencies and familiarizing myself with the bus system in the Phoenix metro area. During my public transportation excursion I happened to stop in at a gas station/convenience store that had a "Help Wanted" sign on the door. I knew I was going to be working for Motorola, providing I passed the BATB tests, but I didn't know how soon that would be. I needed something temporary that would get me an income *now*. So at that gas station, completely on the spur of the moment, I chose to trust my instincts, which told me it was right to fill out an application.

I then went on my merry way, trying to find my way around this completely unfamiliar city, using a public transportation system that did not even come close to comparing with the quality of the public transportation system in Portland. To put it mildly — the bus system in Phoenix sucked! I don't know what it's like now, but in the year 2000 it was pretty terrible. So I decided I'd have to take it in stride and just allow for plenty of time to get where I needed to go.

That afternoon I went in for my interview at Kelly Services, and I also did the aptitude tests. That all went well, and they told me that the soonest they could get me in at Motorola would be July 18th — two weeks (an eternity) away. They then told me where I needed to be on July 5th at 8:00 in the morning to take the BATB tests. Since I had complete confidence in my ability to pass those tests, I knew I was set. The only thing I needed now was something that would get me an income during the next two weeks. (Do you remember the "Now Hiring" sign at the gas station? And my little "intuitive nudge" that told me to fill out an application? It turned out that I was right to trust my intuition, because my phone rang right after I took the BATB test on July 5th, and the owner of that gas station proved to be an incredibly kind man who gave me a break and hired me temporarily, even though he was really looking for a permanent employee.)

The following day was the Fourth of July and pretty much one of the worst days of my life. I had what can only be described as a breakdown. It was awful. I felt absolutely alone and miserably lonely. It was a holiday and I was not able to reach any of the people that I tried to call — and I tried calling everybody! I called Kim, but no one answered, so I left a message asking her to call me back on my cell, and I left my cell number on the off chance that she had lost it. That would explain why I hadn't heard from her since she had dropped me off on Sunday. I was kind of surprised that she hadn't called to check on me. She had told me more than once that if I needed anything I was to call. Oh boy, did I need to hear her voice right then! But she never called me back. I had never felt so alone in all my life. I cried and I cried. I cried so hard that my throat was raw and my eyes were swollen almost shut. I was so lonely and afraid and very, very depressed. I couldn't help thinking, "If I was still with Jeff I wouldn't be feeling this way. At least I wouldn't be alone." I had an incredibly strong urge to pick up the phone and call him. I knew he was waiting for that, it being a holiday and so soon after I had left. I'm sure he was just waiting for me to call and beg to come home. Looking back, I can see just how strong I had become during that week. It would have been easy to give up just then and go back to the life I was familiar with and the hometown that I loved. It wasn't 1000 degrees outside in Portland. It wasn't ugly and brown in Portland. Portland wasn't a great big "I don't know what's going to happen next." Jeff would have welcomed me back and we would have done the Honeymoon Phase of our relationship once again, which would have been nice. In Portland I wouldn't have been alone in a dumpy motel room in a bad part of town on a holiday that was meant to be shared and celebrated with other people.

> *Yes, but in Portland you would never know when a fist full of your hair was going to be ripped out of your head. Yeah, in Portland you wouldn't be alone, but you also would never know when you were going to be screamed at and called a whore. You wouldn't be alone, but you would still be indescribably lonely. Have*

> you forgotten already why you left? Have you forgotten that it was only a matter of time before you were dead at his hands? Have you forgotten what it was like to be terrified of the man that you love? Have you forgotten how much it hurts to be deliberately hurt by the man you love? Have you already forgotten all of the pain in that relationship? Have you already forgotten that he was not willing to work on making that relationship a healthy one? Have you forgotten that he made you responsible for his happiness? Have you forgotten that he refused to take responsibility for his own happiness? And, oh yeah, while we're at it, have you forgotten your decision to take responsibility for YOUR happiness? Jeez, it's only been one week! And not only that, look at how well things are going! You are doing good! Snap out of it! You can give up now if you choose to, but you will regret it for the rest of your short, miserable life if you do.

That thought brought me up short. What was I doing to myself? Was this where I wanted to stay? I was very good at self-pity. Did I need more practice at it? No. I needed to practice finding happiness wherever I could. I realized that what I needed to practice was actually looking for happiness! Happiness was easy when things were going well. This day things didn't seem to be going as well as I would have liked them to. Well, guess what! Here was a perfect opportunity to *practice* creating a healthy life for myself.

Guess what I did next. I'll give you three guesses. Yep, I pulled out my stack of quotes to remind myself of all that I had learned over the last week. As I looked through them all and read the messages I found right there in my hands, I realized that my sponge had dried completely out again. So I concentrated on looking for things to be grateful for. And I found them. Right there in the middle of my loneliness and depression, I looked for and I found things to be grateful for. I had a roof over my head, I had met some really awesome people who had kept me from ending up on the streets of Phoenix, I was able to talk to my children any time I wanted to (when I could reach them!), I was not going hungry, there was an air conditioner in my room, and on and on and on. I looked for and I found things that I was genuinely grateful for. And I began to feel better. I was still lonesome and down, but nothing like before. And I did not have even a shred of an urge to call Jeff left anywhere in me. God is good—and I am still alive to tell about it!

I then turned on the television. My choices were between soap operas and Montel Williams. I figured that since my own life was basically one giant soap opera, I really didn't need to watch them on TV, too, so I picked Montel. It was a show about miracles, of all things. It was just what I needed at that particular moment in time—a reminder that I could believe in miracles. And hadn't I just read the Albert Einstein quote about miracles not five minutes earlier? He said, "There are two ways to look at the world: one is as if nothing is a miracle, and the other is as if everything is a miracle." Watching Montel that day did a lot to rewet my sponge, but what came on after that was even more helpful. Sidney Poitier happened to be on *Oprah* that day, talking about what his life was like when he moved to New York City. He was 15 years old and he had $3.00 in his pocket when he arrived in New York. He didn't know anyone in the city and he had no place to stay. He didn't even know how to dial a telephone. How appropriate it was for me to be watching this particular show on this particular day! It was perfect, and it is things like this that have convinced me over the last years that everything happens for a reason and that there is no such thing as coincidence. This show came on just when I needed its message the most, and what I got from it was this:

> *If a young black man, in that era — when blacks were literally considered inferior — could arrive in New York City with nothing and proceed to take his life as far as he has, then I can damn well do anything I put my mind to!*

This day — Independence Day — was the last time I ever seriously considered going back to Jeff. Yes, I did experience a few more bouts of loneliness and depression after this episode, but none of those ever came close to the intensity of this one. I can say with complete certainty that the reason for this is that I continually reminded myself to look at what was ahead of me, at what I had to look forward to, at what I wanted to create for myself. Every time I found myself feeling sorry for myself for any reason, I practiced looking for things that I could be grateful for *right then and there*, and then I would turn my attention to what I *wanted* to experience in my life. I would deliberately remind myself that:

> *Where I place my attention,*
> *I am placing my Intention.*

Practice, practice, and more practice. In fact, I'm still practicing, and since I am a human being, therefore I'm not perfect and sometimes I do still get stuck on what I don't want instead of what I do want, I will be practicing until the day I die. But my life is so much more enjoyable now that I know that I'm responsible for every bit of it and that I can create whatever I choose to create for myself.

Eight days after climbing on a Greyhound bus and running for my very life, I realized that I was much better off looking at it as just the opposite. When I ran *from* Portland, I was running *toward* a life that I would never have been capable of imagining for myself if I had never felt it to be necessary to run in the first place. And this is the *upward* spiral that I have been experiencing ever since.

This journey was a profound experience for me, and I feel very honored and blessed to have been able to share it with you in this way, and I thank you for travelling it with me!

So if, when you picked up this book, you were a person who had been a victim, or if you were a person who has made unhealthy choices in your past, or if you were a person who felt stuck in a bad or unhealthy situation, or if you were a person with a Dream and no idea how to reach it—you now have some tools available to you, along with living proof that they work if you work them!

And please think of this… you do not have to be a victim of domestic violence to use these principles to change your life! I have told my story from the perspective and experiences of a victim of domestic violence because that was who I was. But anyone can do this! If you have something in your life that you'd like to change, you can change it at any time that you choose to change it. But it has to be you doing the changing! My story is just a great example of the *process* of catching myself in the habits of thought that would create Hell for me, and then creating new, more powerful and life-giving thoughts of the kind of life that I *wanted* to experience.

I cannot recommend *Building Your Field of Dreams* highly enough to anyone who's ready to begin making that

Chapter

shift in direction that can get them to a whole new place. I know I've said this before, but I'm going to say it one last time: That book saved my life, and if you want to know who you really are and how you can make your life what you want it to be, it is my sincere opinion that you can find those things for yourself in its pages if you choose to do so. Find yourself a copy of *Building Your Field of Dreams* and discover just what YOU are capable of accomplishing!

Pop Your Paradigm!

Chapter 12

A Happy Ending?

*"When we are in harmony with the Truth of our Being,
we feel fulfilled."
~ Mary Manin Morrissey*

So? Were you able to spot the tyrant as it showed up? (WHAM!!!) And the "loving friend," too? And what about the various Swords of Truth? Good for you!

I love the quote above, because it speaks so well to this whole story, and to what popping our paradigms can do for us. The paradigm blocks us from fully aligning with the Truth of our Being. The Sword of Truth cuts right through that paradigm — it pops the paradigm and renders it powerless. And this leaves us free to align ourselves with the Truth of who we really are. And who are we really? The "Truth of our Being" IS the "loving and supportive friend." When we can learn to recognize the tyrant — the paradigm — and neutralize it, this clears the way for us to allow ourselves to be our own friend, to get "in harmony with the Truth of our Being." And when we do that, we truly do feel fulfilled.

In the years since I stepped off that bus and into a whole new experience of my life I have had many awesome and wonderful adventures, and in the midst of each one of those adventures I have had to deal with the tyrant. I've had to pop that paradigm and get out of my own way if I wanted to reach whatever Dream I happened to be going for. And in some cases, I must admit, the tyrant got the better of me and I remained in my Fear for too long and lost my Dream. But it has ALL been a wonderful experience of learning and growing into the woman I am today.

The woman I am today IS happy. But is this the end of the story? I think not! Every day is a beginning. Every new idea is a beginning, and every beginning produces another opportunity for growth and becoming MORE of who I want to be. Each beginning is an opportunity to create new experiences that I want to live and love. And in every moment of all of that I get to choose what I'm going to do with it. THIS is living a happy and fulfilled life, popping that paradigm and working in harmony with my own Self to create the life I want to be living, rather than being at the mercy of that giant thumb, the tyrant.

So now go and live your adventure, and remember to keep your Sword at the ready… and when the tyrant shows up (and it will!), *Pop Your Paradigm!*

> Thank you so much for spending this time with me!
> God bless you!
> Love,
> Sandi

> *"The way my life is right now is a direct result of my habits of thought."*
> *— Me —*

The Shifting of a Paradigm

Paradigm, oh paradigm,
You've had control of my life
You've stopped me from having
The things that I want
And you've given me
Struggle and strife.
You took control away from me
Because I didn't know you were there
You've used your sly little tricks in my mind
To keep me stuck right here.

But guess what! I see you now
And I'm watching your power fade
As I make my choices in spite of you
I can see my Dreams *already made*
I'm not *really* destined to live
Only lack and limitation
I am meant to live *real* life
Not just a hollow imitation.

So now I know that I'm ready
To send you on your way
To get unstuck from littleness
To look at you and say,
"I thank you for the lessons learned
And for protecting me as you are.
I'll take over from here now, though,
Because *I* am more powerful than *you*, by far."

By
Sandra A. Daly
Copyright 2009

In Gratitude

There are so many people and things that I appreciate! Where should I begin? I think I'll start with my history. I can't help but look at my history with appreciation, for without that history I would not be the person I am today, living the Joy-full life that I'm living today.

I would like to acknowledge, and say a giant, "Thank you!" to the following people: My wonderful husband, Rick, who loves me for who I am and would never ask me to be something I'm not; Mary Manin Morrissey, for living her life and sharing with the world all the things that she has learned for herself; Nick Ligidakis and Inkwell Productions, for making the publishing of this book possible; and the owners and staff of Caruso Turley Scott Inc., for all the wonderful support and encouragement you have given me over the years, when you certainly didn't have to – you cannot know how much that has meant to me. To all of you – thank you! There are, of course, countless others in my life that I appreciate, some of whom can be found in this book, and others who may have had a passing, but powerful, influence on me. I love and appreciate you all!

Currently, I find myself the most influenced by, learning from, and appreciating tremendously the following people: Mary Manin Morrissey, Jerry and Esther Hicks, Bob Proctor, Paul Martinelli, Dr. Wayne Dyer, Sydney Chase, David and Kristin Morelli, and Neale Donald Walsch.